INTERFACE

PEOPLE, MACHINES, DESIGN

MUSEUM OF APPLIED ARTS
AND SCIENCES

First published 2014
Museum of Applied Arts and Sciences
500 Harris St, Ultimo, NSW 2007
Interface: people, machines, design
is published in conjuction with
the exhibition of the same name
at the Powerhouse Museum
15 August 2014–11 October 2015.
powerhousemuseum.com/publications

National Library of Australia CIP
ISBN 9781863171601 (paperback)
Bickerstaff, Campbell
Interface: people, machines, design
Information technology – History
Computer interfaces – History
Computers – History
Other Authors/Contributors:
Stein, Jesse Adams
Byrne, Seamus
Bibliography
Dewey Number: 004

Curator:
Campbell Bickerstaff
Publication Manager and Editor:
Judith Matheson
Additional Editing:
Melanie Cariss and Karla Bo Johnson
Publication Design:
Leuver Design
Rights and Permissions:
Iwona Hetherington
Photography:
Marinco Kojdanovski
and Sotha Bourn
Printed by:
Asia Pacific Offset

Printed in China

Museum of Applied Arts and Sciences
is a NSW government cultural institution.

Publication © Museum of
Applied Arts and Sciences

This publication is copyright.
Apart from fair dealing for the
purposes of research, study,
criticism or review, or as otherwise
permitted under the Copyright Act,
no part may be reproduced by any
process without written permission.

All company logos, trademarks
and product names in this
publication remain the property
of their respective owners.

Cover: detail of Safnat telephone,
Museum of Applied Arts and
Sciences collection.

CONTENTS

5	FOREWORD ROSE HISCOCK
6	INTERFACE: PEOPLE, MACHINES, DESIGN CAMPBELL BICKERSTAFF
18	A CONVERSATION WITH MARIO BELLINI CAMPBELL BICKERSTAFF
26	THE THINKING MAN'S FOOD PROCESSOR: DOMESTICITY, GENDER AND THE APPLE II JESSE ADAMS STEIN
32	FAN FRICTION: DESIGN-CENTRIC BATTLE LINES IN THE SMART PHONE AGE SEAMUS BYRNE
39	THE ENTHUSIASTS WE SHAPE OUR TOOLS
75	THE PROFESSIONALS FROM USABILITY TO USER FRIENDLY
111	THE CONSUMERS FORM FOLLOWS EMOTION
168	ENDNOTES
171	PHOTO CREDITS
172	OBJECT ACKNOWLEDGMENTS
173	BIBLIOGRAPHY
174	ABOUT THE CONTRIBUTORS

FOREWORD

The Museum of Applied Arts and Sciences is pleased to present *Interface: people, machines, design*, which brings together aspects of our technology and design collections through a fresh and compelling new narrative. *Interface* is an opportunity to reflect on the past 100 years and to understand the dynamics, context and the people who transformed information technology machines into tools for everyday culture. It is also a chance to look forward. We live in an increasingly complex and interconnected world where the hybrid disciplines of applied arts and sciences will be more relevant to our world than ever before.

With a history spanning more than a century, the Museum is uniquely placed to present an account of information technology design. Throughout most of the 20th century, the Museum acquired radios, televisions, telephones and other domestic appliances as part of its 'electronics' collection. Early calculators and computers — often behemoth mainframes that filled rooms — were also collected under the 'sciences' banner. These strands are merged in *Interface*.

From the mid 1990s the Museum seized the opportunity to rethink these collections and identify and acquire landmark devices. A new generation of curators was acquiring material in order to tell the story of developments in human machine interaction. There was a desire to see beyond the technological; to explore the relationship between the engineered object and its symbolic value to the user and consumer.

The Museum's approach coincided with a time when industrial designers began to take centre stage. It was influential German designer Hartmut Esslinger who turned the old adage "form follows function" on its head with his provocative statement "form follows emotion". Esslinger created a product development team at Apple that was design-led rather than engineering-led. The Museum's collection contains many early technological items that are beautiful and elegant yet their designers remain anonymous to this day. By contrast, contemporary designers, such as Sir Jonathan Ive, are invested with cult status. *Interface* pays homage to designers past and present and explores their philosophies and inspirations.

We are delighted and honoured to present an interview with revered architect and designer Mario Bellini. A pioneer in the field, Bellini's work and influence is evident throughout *Interface*. Essays by curator Campbell Bickerstaff, design academic Jesse Adams Stein and technology journalist Seamus Byrne present different perspectives on the *Interface* theme.

One of the challenges in collecting information technologies is that the rate of obsolescence has accelerated. Technologies are scrapped and thrown away before they have the opportunity to become objects of historical interest. Our curators are attuned to these developments and recognise an item's significance before it disappears.

Presenting *Interface* gave the Museum the opportunity to consider this future significance and the curator, Campbell Bickerstaff, set about acquiring 31 new objects for the exhibition, including Olivetti typewriters and calculators designed by pioneers Bellini and Marcello Nizzoli, examples of 1960s Braun consumer electronics designed by Dieter Rams, and a number of first generation Apple products by Esslinger, Ives and others. A rare Apple 1 computer, the first commercial product built by the fledgling Apple computer company in the mid 1970s, also features. Of a production run of 200, only about 50 original Apple 1s are known to have survived and the Museum was fortunate to acquire one in 2010. It is one of a number of internationally significant information technology devices from our collection that feature in this book.

Interface: people, machines, design represents what the Museum does best. It is an outstanding example of the Museum's focus upon the hybrid disciplines of arts and sciences as increasingly relevant to our world and a valuable resource for the scientists, engineers and designers of the future.

ROSE HISCOCK
DIRECTOR
MUSEUM OF APPLIED ARTS
AND SCIENCES
SYDNEY, AUSTRALIA

INTERFACE

PEOPLE MACHINES DESIGN

BY CAMPBELL BICKERSTAFF

INTERFACE EXAMINES THE APPLICATION OF DESIGN TO INFORMATION TECHNOLOGY PRODUCTS FROM THE LATE 19TH TO THE EARLY 21ST CENTURIES. THIS ESSAY PROVIDES AN HISTORICAL OVERVIEW OF THE PERIOD AND CONSIDERS HOW A HANDFUL OF COMPANIES, THEIR VISIONARY FOUNDERS AND THE DESIGNERS THEY EMPLOYED, MADE COMPLICATED TECHNOLOGY APPEALING AND EASY TO USE.

The Olivetti TE300 teleprinter was designed by Ettore Sottsass in 1968.

The smart phone, a device first launched on the market in 2007, is now the go-to information technology machine for the masses. As of 2013, production of smart phones worldwide surpassed that of its predecessor, the mobile phone. Smart phones have dominated the US market since 2011 and the international shift has been driven by new markets in China, India and Indonesia[1]. Global domination took just six years.

Why and how do these devices appeal to us? Firstly, a smart phone is a mobile device that can make and receive phone calls and text messages almost anywhere in the world. But it has much greater computing capability and connectivity than its predecessor, the mobile phone. It can send and receive emails. It can take photos and video footage. It is a personal digital assistant and a portable media player. All of this technology and more can be operated via a highly responsive, high resolution touch screen that is both simple and appealing to use. This remarkable device is small enough to fit into the palm of the user's hand or in their pocket. It is, above all, a lifestyle accessory.

The intuitive nature of its operation has led to our rapid embrace of smart phone technology. The smart phone is an incredibly complicated device, and yet the user needs no special skills or understanding of the technology to use it. How we reached this point in human-machine interaction or 'interface' is the focus of this book.

Human-machine interface operates through a loop of input and feedback. The user performs a task and the machine offers a sign of some kind that the task has been performed successfully. This sensory feedback (see / feel / hear) is both satisfying and reassuring and responds to a basic human need. When machines were mechanical, the link between the action and the device was physical and so was the feedback. Hitting a typewriter key to type a letter or adjusting a tuning knob on a radio to get the clearest signal provides immediate sensory feedback. The advent of computers heralded a dislocation from a physical input / output system that challenged designers to explore new methods of interface.

The smart phone had many forerunners, for example, the personal digital assistants of the 1990s (PalmPilot and Newton) but they did not resonate with consumers. However these early products created an important legacy that later industrial designers built upon to develop the smart phone.

Such developmental threads are echoed in other products — from calculators to computers, typewriters to toys — leading to the evolution of the information technologies we enjoy today.

These threads of successful and not-so-successful design methods, approaches, influences and ideals are shared by different companies and designers, in different parts of the world, at different times. *Interface* extracts those threads and pays homage to the ideas, the designers, the companies and the devices that preceded the extraordinary information technology that is now part of our everyday lives.

Interface examines the application of design to information technology products. It considers how a handful of companies made complicated technology appealing and easy to use; what they did, effectively, was look at what you do, think about what you need and create what you want. Interface is also about the visionaries who founded some of the great consumer product companies of the 20th century and how the designers and engineers they hired found a means of imparting their ideals into the products they designed.

Whether a typewriter, a calculator or a computer, all technological devices undergo different stages of development. Technology specialist David Liddle identifies three distinct phases of acceptance: an enthusiast phase, a professional phase and a consumer phase[2]. Each phase frames the growing consumption of a new technology and in turn creates a new set of demands on the designers of that technology.

Interface examines the ability of designers to build on our engagement with these devices throughout each phase. The contribution of a small pool of exemplary designers to the evolution of forms in industrial design is substantial, and the book reflects on the links between those product forms and other arts.

Interface draws on the Museum's extensive collection to examine the design process of information technology products developed from the late 19th century to the early 21st century, when smart phone and tablet technology marks the end of a chapter in product development.

DESIGN IN THE AGE OF MASS PRODUCTION

Through the mid to late 19th century, new industrial manufacturing methods made it possible to mass produce everyday objects for rapidly expanding consumer markets. Yet these new manufacturing methods were often adopted without consideration of their implications for materials and forms. Rather than exploring the benefits that the new technologies offered, designers revisited previous styles — Renaissance, Baroque, Rococo and Empire among others — as they slipped in and out of fashion. Product design seemed to flounder in this period; mass-produced objects were often grotesque and ill-conceived. However, it was a fertile time for the gestation of ideas about what design in the new machine age should encompass.

In Britain, William Morris (1834–96) and John Ruskin (1819–1900) were among those who defended the role of the artisan against authorless mass production methods, as crafts workers increasingly saw their livelihoods threatened by the new industrial methods. But it was the voices of those who decried the application of unnecessarily ornate flourishes to modern, functional products that began to gain momentum. At the same time, ideas about the relationship between skills, tools, materials and function began to coalesce and an understanding of their influence on product development took shape.

Christopher Dresser (1834–1904) was an outspoken proponent of modern design. Often considered the first independent industrial designer, Dresser was studious in his efforts to understand the new techniques of production and, most importantly, to consider a product in terms of its use, manufacture and symbolic value. His products — fabrics, metalwork and ceramics — were successful because they had been formed through a design method that considered the user, the materials, the manufacturing process and the society in which it would be consumed.

In Germany, an association of architects, designers and industrialists was established in 1907 to support modern industrial design. The Deutscher Werkbund considered design in terms of the materials and technologies suited to industrial production, and viewed ornament as unnecessary and indulgent. The Werkbund exhibited new forms that highlighted these preoccupations, as well as issues of standardisation, economies of production and designing aesthetically pleasing goods for mass production[3].

Information technology design visionaries.
Top left: Adriano Olivetti.
Bottom left: Steve Wozniak and Steve Jobs.
Bottom right: Artur and Erwin Braun.

At the same time, major advances in technologies such as electricity, telephony and radio created a market for new products and devices that, by their very nature, were nothing like existing tools and machines.

IDEALS, DEMOCRACY, ACCESS AND PRODUCT DESIGN

In the 20th century leading information technology companies, such as Olivetti, Braun and Apple, aspired to high ideals, practised corporate benevolence and believed that their products had the ability to democratise the workplace and sometimes the wider society.

Olivetti was a small Italian family business established in the first decade of the 20th century by the engineer Camillo Olivetti (1868–1943). Camillo wanted to change people's lives. He wanted to engineer a great Italian typewriter, employ people and contribute to the emerging modern Italy. Camillo's son Adriano Olivetti (1901–60) was appointed general manager in 1933.

Illustrating three phases of adoption: the Blickensderfer 6 typewriter; the IBM Selectric; and the Olivetti Valentine.

Adriano was enamoured by the modernist aesthetic and had, in the years previous to his appointment, visited the US to observe modern industrial practices. He immediately set about recruiting the best designers and architects. Under his leadership the company became one of the first Italian manufacturers to consider the links between the means of production of a new technological product and its appearance and cultural role in the contemporary environment. Adriano believed that "design is a question of substance, not just form" and that it was a "tool a company uses through its products, graphics and architecture to convey an image that is not just simply appearance but a tangible reflection of a way of being and operating"[4].

Braun was established in Germany in the 1920s by engineer Max Braun (1890–1951). His unexpected death in 1951 handed control to his sons Artur (1925–2013), an engineer, and Erwin (1921–92), a business graduate. Together they quickly set about revitalising Braun, forging alliances with some of Germany's most influential and progressive people including the film director and art historian Dr Fritz Eichler and the industrial designer Wilhelm Wagenfeld (1900–90). This team formed an alliance with the Hochschule fur Gestaltung (Hfg) school of design in Ulm, which had recently been established to train a new generation of designers (with a purpose and curriculum similar to the Bauhaus of the 1920s). The HfG dismissed the idea of the intuitive individualist as creator; students were encouraged to work collaboratively across disciplines, apply scientific analysis to dilemmas and explore functionalist design solutions. Two of the lecturers, Hans Gugelot (1920–65) and Otl Aicher (1921–91), were engaged by the Braun brothers as consultants to rethink the design of Braun radios, gramophones and electric razors. Within eight months this team had succeeded in reshaping Braun's entire product line — replacing any trace of the dated and distinguishing features of the previous decades with new materials, finishes and shapes.

In 1955 Dieter Rams (1932–) joined Braun as an architect and interior designer. Rams has articulated his belief that good design and democracy are intertwined[5]. This relationship is complex and not particularly literal, but the basic premise is that democratic products embody democratic values such as freedom, mobility, accessibility, simplicity, affordability, connectedness and transparency. As Germany recovered from chaos in the aftermath of World War II, Rams sought to apply these democratic ideals to his designs for Braun.

The principles of US-based company Apple were ingrained at its genesis by the company's founders Steve Jobs (1955–2011) and Steve Wozniak (1950–). They established Apple to build computer technology, not principally for gain, but for what they perceived as its social and ethical reach[6]. At the time the company was started in the mid 1970s, the future of the computer lay in the hands of a few — the powerful industrial and military complex. The first Apple computer, the Apple I, was instead designed as a computer for people, a personal computer.

Apple's skill was in reimagining technologies struggling in their pre-consumer phase (the personal computer, the digital media player and the smart phone) to create successful products like the Macintosh, iPod and iPhone. By resolving issues of usability and sourcing new materials to make them possible, Apple broadened the acceptance and usefulness of these technologies.

THREE PHASES OF ADOPTION

As David Liddle has argued, throughout the 20th century new technologies passed through the three stages of adoption: an enthusiast phase, a professional phase and a consumer phase[7]. In the first phase enthusiasts or early adopters engage with a new technology for its own sake, regardless of how complicated or impractical it may be. Using the example of typewriters, in the beginning they were somewhat baffling machines (even to today's eyes), not based on any existing products. They were used by the few who were enthusiastic enough to see beyond any shortcomings. These early adopters embraced a new mechanised way of writing which offered uniformity, reliability, and accuracy.

As this new product was tested by people in real conditions and judged on new criteria, the marketplace began to prefer some typewriter designs over others. Those preferred elements of design gradually became the norm and were copied by other manufacturers. For example, there were two popular keyboard configurations in early typewriters but the QWERTY keyboard eventually prevailed. Recent studies suggest the input from telegraph operators

Science fiction often inspired new forms of interface. A form of gesture control is featured in this scene from *The Day the Earth Stood Still* (1951).

(early adopters of typewriters) was applied to the layout of the keys[8].

Early adopters saw the typewriter's potential to save labour and costs and recognised a need within business and the wider community that it could satisfy. Developing the technology beyond the enthusiast phase and turning it into a product which has a commercial use is the second stage in the product's adoption. This professional phase is signalled by a change in priorities. As Liddle explains, someone gets "a clever idea about how they are going to do something really practical with it"[9]. During this phase new design values apply. Reliability, performance, useability and price become critical factors.

Typewriters, for example, went from cumbersome machines which jammed and had parts that obscured documents during their creation, among other foibles, to finely machined and assembled devices with well weighted keys that flew to the platen with satisfaction.

By the early 20th century the typewriter had made its way from the laboratory into the office but its design was still very much dictated by its function. As the century progressed the enabling technology employed in typewriters moved from mechanical to electrical to electronic. Electric typewriters were commercially produced as early as the 1920s, but it was the IBM Selectric launched in 1961 that dominated the market for 20 years.

Over the same period, the portable typewriter was reaching a consumer market — the third stage of adoption. Olivetti in particular produced affordable and colourful new models that took the typewriter out of the office and into the home. By the 1980s typewriters were transitioning into electronic word processors. This change coincided with the rise of microcomputers in the workplace and led to the eventual demise of the typewriter in modern offices.

Only a few decades earlier, the suggestion that a computer would be used or needed by ordinary working people, other than engineers, was science fiction. In the 1950s computers were room-filling, number-crunching machines operated by

Scientific research also contributed to the development of interface. This is an early prototype of the computer mouse.

men in white coats. Creating a computer that was efficient and small enough to sit on an employee's desk took decades of developments in computer architecture, languages, operating systems and hardware. But what had the greatest impact on the computer's adoption was the work of a few people who developed and refined its input and output features, the human-computer interface.

In the development of human-computer interface there were two crucial innovations: the mouse and the graphical user interface. The design of the mouse and the system it operated within took a leap in thinking in the late 1960s. The original computer mouse was designed and built by engineers Doug Engelbart (1925–2013) and Bill English at the Stanford Research Institute in California and was named the 'X-Y Position Indicator for a Display System'[10]. When the user moved the mouse in the real world, the pointer on the computer screen moved in the virtual world, mimicking the user's movements. In this way, the mouse created a powerful interaction between people and computers.

Another Californian research facility, Xerox PARC founded in 1971, developed and predicted key technologies that would be the cornerstone of the personal computer systems we now use, notably the graphical user interface (GUI)[11]. Basically a GUI substitutes symbols for typed commands, making it much easier and more intuitive for the user to tell the computer what to do. The GUI human-computer interface was part of a broader shift from written communication to a new visual literacy in the world. Computer scientist Alan Kay (1940–), who developed the SmallTalk computer language at Xerox, believed that computers should be simple enough for a child to use[12]. Xerox incorporated a GUI into its Alto computer in the 1970s, and although the company was not successful in commercialising this platform it nevertheless paved the way for the computer interface we use today.

It was a team from Apple that successfully commercialised the mouse and the GUI. Steve Jobs first saw the Alto in December 1979. He was transfixed and immediately understood that the mouse and GUI were the tools non-computer users needed to interact with a computer[13]. Apple quickly established two computer development teams who would work on a GUI with mouse system for business (Lisa) and home use (which eventually became the Macintosh personal computer).

Of this period, information scientist John Carroll recently wrote: "All these threads of development in computer science pointed to the same conclusion: The way forward for computing entailed understanding and better empowering users. These diverse forces of need and opportunity converged around 1980, focusing a huge burst of human energy, and creating a highly visible interdisciplinary project."[14]

During the consumer phase a device's features and capabilities become intuitive to the user. For example, it is now rare to see someone unfamiliar with a mouse and its operation. Freed from the constraints placed on them previously — manuals and training are unnecessary — consumers embrace the device and the uptake accelerates. The machine and the experience of using it has been successfully humanised.

A product can enter the consumer phase in different ways, from superficial (cladding) to complete rethinking and re-engineering of the device and its use.

Avant-garde art movements and artists influenced Olivetti's product design. Abstract painter Alberto Magnelli was the brother of Olivetti designer Aldo Magnelli.

For example, in the 1950s transistor technology enabled radios to become personal and portable. The new products appealed to an emerging youth market who were listening to the sounds of early rock 'n' roll. In the 1980s Sony created a new product category with the Walkman — a cassette machine without a record function or a speaker that instead offered portable high fidelity music of the user's choice accessed through headphones. In the 2000s Apple's iPod digital media player integrated extraordinarily well with a desktop computer application and internet service (iTunes), enabling the user to buy and load music into the device, up to a thousand songs, and access this information through simple controls.

To recap on the smart phone, this technology's enthusiast phase was the personal digital assistants of the 1990s (PalmPilot, Newton) — mobile computing devices with a poor user interface. Early smart phone devices, such as the Blueberry, were embraced by business people and professionals but did not fully capture the consumer market. This was followed by the iPhone, a device with a screen-based interface where the dynamic screen images seemingly respond to touch and gesture. Inertial scrolling, audio prompts and multi-fingered gesture enhance the experience of being connected to the machine in an apparently effortless way.

FORM FOLLOWS EMOTION

Product design is invested with layers of meaning formed from the observations, preferences, actions and emotions of the designer. Throughout the 20th and early 21st centuries, a handful of designers have excelled at distilling these layers into appealing forms.

When formulating their vision, the designer draws upon a pool of concepts and disciplines, cultural and political influences. Painting, sculpture, architecture and graphic design, among others, have made a substantial contribution to the evolution of form in industrial design. At Olivetti, for example, the company's progressive founders enlisted Bauhaus and Italian polytechnic graduates who were skilled painters, graphic artists, architects and exhibit designers. Olivetti designers were also involved in various avant-garde art movements, such as futurism, which celebrated modernity and the machine and embraced new materials and forms. Futurist ideology influenced Olivetti's elevation of industrial products from everyday objects to emblems of a new civilisation. Olivetti was extraordinarily successful at identifying people who were able to translate their skills as visual artists into industrial design for business machines.

Marcello Nizzoli (1887–1969) was a painter influenced by futurism who joined Olivetti in the early 1930s as a graphic designer, however his talents were soon applied to the development of calculators and typewriters. Nizzoli went on to become Olivetti's chief design consultant in 1936, and he remained in that role until 1958. His designs from this period draw heavily on modernism and the organic fluid forms of artists such as the sculptor Henry Moore.

Ettore Sottsass (1917–2007) was another extraordinary figure in Italian and international design. The architect and industrial designer took on the role of chief design consultant at Olivetti following Nizzoli in 1958. In the 1960s he introduced a pop art aesthetic to Olivetti, launching the Valentine typewriter, which, with its flowing bright red plastic form, appears far removed from a piece of office equipment.

Olivetti's chief design consultant from 1963 to 1991 was Mario Bellini (1935–), one of the most celebrated designers of the past 50 years. A 1959 architecture graduate of the Milan Polytechnic, Bellini has worked across the fields of urban planning and architecture as well as product and furniture design. Rather than highlighting a product's technical dimensions, his designs are playful and inviting. The Divisumma 18 portable calculator, which Bellini designed for Olivetti in 1973,

This Olivetti poster was designed by Walter Ballmer in 1971. Ballmer also designed the Olivetti logo in 1970.

is a good example. The calculator has a synthetic rubber keypad, with gracefully elevated nipple-shaped keys, that is sensuous but also practical.

In his design method Bellini seldom made use of drawing; preferring to experiment and develop models through a dialogue that refined how a user might experience the product. His approach considered both the tactile appeal of a product and the user's emotional response to it. This aspect of Bellini's design philosophy became highly influential; it was an attitude other great 20th century product designers understood and employed.

It was German designer Hartmut Esslinger (1944–) who used the phrase "form follows emotion", an adaptation of architect Louis Sullivan's edict that "form follows function", to elucidate his guiding principle for frog design, the design agency he founded in the late 1960s[15]. While Esslinger may have turned the old philosophy on its head to provoke his audience, it was particularly suited to the age of the microprocessor because the integration of solid state circuitry into office equipment eliminated the mechanical features of machines. Designers were no longer simply cladding what the engineers came up with. Some designers were more adept than others at navigating a path through this transition to develop new forms.

In 1983 Esslinger became design consultant for Apple[16]. Of this time Esslinger has written, "... I urged Steve (Jobs) to rethink Apple's existing design process and the way it placed designers at the mercy of engineering. I told him that,

Are smart phones the new worry beads? As a device to occupy the hands and mind, the smart phone is now pervasive, demanding the user's attention and usurping simpler diversions.

in my opinion, Apple needed one design leader and one team reporting directly to him, and design had to be involved years ahead of any actual product development in Apple's strategic planning."[17]

Apple's Senior Vice President of Design since 1997 is English designer Sir Jonathan Ive (1967–). His early designs for Apple drew on Bellini's approach: small details become playful elements that distract from the technology of the product. Ive has spoken about creating an emotional response to his designs. For example, the form of his first industrial design for Apple, the MessagePad, evolved after he "discovered that by allowing the user to fiddle with the retractable pen and play with the pop-up lid, we could elicit the more abstract emotions of intrigue and surprise that would make Lindy (the project name for MessagePad) seem personal and precious."[18] This design philosophy to involve the user in an unfolding narrative of product features carried through to the iMac, iPod and MacBook.

Ive also appreciated and applied the principles that underscored previous great design legacies such as that of Dieter Rams. Since 2000 Ive's designs for Apple and Rams' designs for Braun display a strong resemblance in form, finish, materials and treatments. Ive's admiration for Rams' design output is evident in his products for Apple, while Rams has said that "Apple is one of only a handful of companies existing today that design products according to Rams' ten principles of good design"[19]. Rams has spoken of his desire to present a product's function clearly and communicate a sense of purity in form (simple shapes, colour and a unified use of materials). These elements are echoed in Ive's output today.

By making information technology machines intriguing, beautiful and functional, talented designers, and the visionary industrialists who hired them, created vital tools for everyday culture. They responded to the challenges presented by new technologies. However their focus was not on the technology, which is increasingly out of view, but on what it can do for the user.

In a recent overview of the history of human-computer interface (a term first coined in the 1980s) John Carroll argues: "The concept of usability has been re-articulated and reconstructed almost continually, and has become increasingly rich and intriguingly problematic. Usability now often subsumes qualities like fun, wellbeing, collective efficacy, aesthetic tension, enhanced creativity, flow, support for human development, and others. A more dynamic view of usability is one of a programmatic objective that should and will continue to develop as our ability to reach further toward it improves."[20]

With their minimalist appearance and optimal applications, the smart phone and tablet computer represent the end of one chapter in portable computer product development and the beginnings of another. What designers are able to shape in the form of interactive design through screen images and surface gesture control will have its limits. The interface may move into the space between the user and the device, where tracking and gesture may be manipulated. What is certain is that the more we use new information technology products, the more we change the way we do things to accommodate them. This technological determinism is best articulated in the quote attributed to Marshall McLuhan: "We shape our tools and then our tools shape us"[21].

A CONVERSATION WITH MARIO BELLINI

MARIO BELLINI WAS OLIVETTI'S CHIEF DESIGN CONSULTANT FROM 1963 TO 1991 AND ONE OF THE GREAT PRODUCT DESIGNERS OF THE 20TH CENTURY. HIS DESIGNS AND HIS INFLUENCE FEATURE THROUGHOUT THIS BOOK. CURATOR CAMPBELL BICKERSTAFF SPOKE TO MARIO BELLINI BY PHONE IN MARCH 2014. THIS IS AN EDITED TRANSCRIPT OF THEIR CONVERSATION.

CAMPBELL BICKERSTAFF Mr Bellini, thank you for agreeing to talk to me. I would like start at the beginning — when did you realise that you wanted to pursue a career in design and why?

MARIO BELLINI Since my early years I have been drawing, designing and following my father's family of basic talent. It was natural to me. And at the age of eight, if I remember well, I built my first little house in the garden with real bricks. And I used to paint and create short colour cartoon films, with coloured ink, for my cousins.

At the end of high school, I had to decide which university to enter. I remember well that moment. Finally, after examining the different kind of university programs, I decided for architecture, because it seemed to me the right balance between art and technique, between creativity, freedom, and science, between imagining and realising things.

CB A prevalent theme within the early 20th century design teaching and practice is that good design can promote or elevate democracy. Did this philosophy influence your design thought and methods?

MB Let's see. I wouldn't put it that way, even if I was swimming in the same waters. I was spontaneously enthusiastic about creating, innovating things, using knowledge, using available technologies, and looking to other technologies, even science and engineering.

I always wanted to understand, to do it better, and to go further, when designing something. Being an architect I had a chance to spend a couple of years in La Rinascente, a very famous department store in Milan, which also had offices for creating some of their production objects.

And that was a seminal experience for me. I discovered the way you can use any technology around you, without being the one who created the technology, and put yourself in the historical flow of things. When you design a table or a chair or a lamp, you don't start a new world, you enter into a process that has been done for millennia.

I never like to consider design as something new, which started a few decades ago. Instead of calling it design, design, design, in Italian, design is a magic word. For you it means something obvious, it means to design, that's it, following the Latin roots of *disegno*.

And that's why I never put myself in that mode. This is my point, if you are here to do something, you must do it well, at the highest level you can, until it speaks for itself and looks right. That's always been my imperative.

CB You mention objects like chairs that have been around for thousands of years, but when you came to Olivetti and designed an object, for example the portable calculator, that really didn't exist before, you were working in a vacuum. Where did you start from?

MB Yes. I can tell you something about that. I instinctively started designing, I don't know, calculators, a couple of years after the experience I told you about. But as I started designing machines, which was totally new for me, I found it natural, because ... have you seen the Antonello da Messina *Annunciata* where the Madonna holds her hands over a sloped book holder, a lectern?

That simple and magic gesture tells you everything. Ever since human beings have been reading or writing, they were doing it on a kind of lectern with a gentle slope. That is much more profound. What is important to consider is who is using the machine, is it for an habitative or working context? That is the point. I never overestimated functionality by itself as a banal 'need'.

In fact, my experience, little by little, started telling me that when you design a machine you think you will have done something extraordinary, but two years later it is old, it is outdated, and you have to do something new. You may feel you have learned the technology, you possess technology, but it's not true, because it's continually flowing and changing and updating.

So at the end, if you understand that, everything goes back to you, to your mind, to your being a human being.

CB Ettore Sottsass once recalled that Olivetti had asked him to design an electric typewriter, but within five, ten years, it was superseded because the microprocessor had come along.

MB Of course. It's a very strange experience, when giving a lecture to students, and you have to say, very cautiously, you know guys, what existed years ago was some very strange machine called the typewriting machine. And they wonder, because today even the idea of a typewriting machine is unbelievable.

CB I want to pick up on that point. You were involved with the introduction of new technologies at a time when the mechanical interface with a device was beginning to disappear.

MB Exactly, that's what I would like to touch on also.

CB How did you retain that desire for people to interact with a device like the typewriter when it no longer gave mechanical feedback?

MB Yes, when I was called by Olivetti to be their consultant, I was doing other things, I was doing furniture, and I was starting some small architecture and so forth. I was there at exactly that moment when the mechanical, but even more, the electromechanical era was fast disappearing, and the new electronic and digital era was entering. That has been my unbelievable challenge and chance, at the same time, and that's why I enjoyed so much doing it, because I had the privilege to invent new typology, new animals, and new objects.

And I never did think to put a new electronic typewriter into something looking like a typewriter, you know? Like an IBM or something. And I put the question to myself — how is it today, how would it be in 30 years, how would this new typewriter be? You know? That was my very big pleasure and satisfaction, to be inventive.

CB Discussions of your work often examine your desire to remove the technological from technology — to be playful — and not threaten the consumer.

MB Okay, you've got it. But first, I didn't like to consider the concept of somebody being a consumer. That was the first strong point. The best way was not to consider that person a consumer but a human being, who had to live and work with those objects, let's call them machines, in a rapidly updating and transforming working environment. And that probably came to me from my architectural background, which was more centred on a general attitude towards man, space, culture, instead of considering a banal relationship between needs and forms, materials and technologies.

I never accepted those banal concepts used by ordinary industrial design. It's an attitude from schools — form follow function, all these things — I found it very banal and used by schools to invent a pedagogy.

CB You have spoken about engaging with the design of a product through model making.

MB Of course.

CB What is it that you experience through this process that helps you modify form?

MB Well, when you design a machine, you might see it instinctually and that will be the best way, but these are things that will then go into the hands of people, over their tables, in front of their chairs, within their working environment.

And they will, for sure, have tactile experiences and physical relationships, not only in the banal way, but also in an emotional way.

And that's why I've always been attracted instinctively by anthropomorphic and zoomorphic attitudes in designing an object. That's because we are anthropomorphic and zoomorphic too, we are very complex and sophisticated beings, with tactile and sensible views and touch and memory. And as such, we can touch much better with objects which are able to give us an emotion, to invite us in relationships more profound than just banally functional, as if you were, I don't know, a helicopter driver, you know?

CB Yes.

MB The origin of the words bureau, bureaucrat, bureaucracy and so on, goes back to the old German language. In medieval times when a man went into a public market to deal money, for example, he was using a simple table, putting a green felt piece of fabric over it, which was called bure. That tells you about the original placement. And that's why I'm so sensible to the deep and profound anthropological roots of our articles.

By using models you anticipate with your hands and your eyes, all trying and modifying and working until you are satisfied, until you feel that's right. It's a way to anticipate and to assure that the experience with the users will actually be a satisfying one.

At the same time, architects and artists use modelling. They do preparatory

The synthetic rubber keypad of the Divisumma 18 portable calculator.

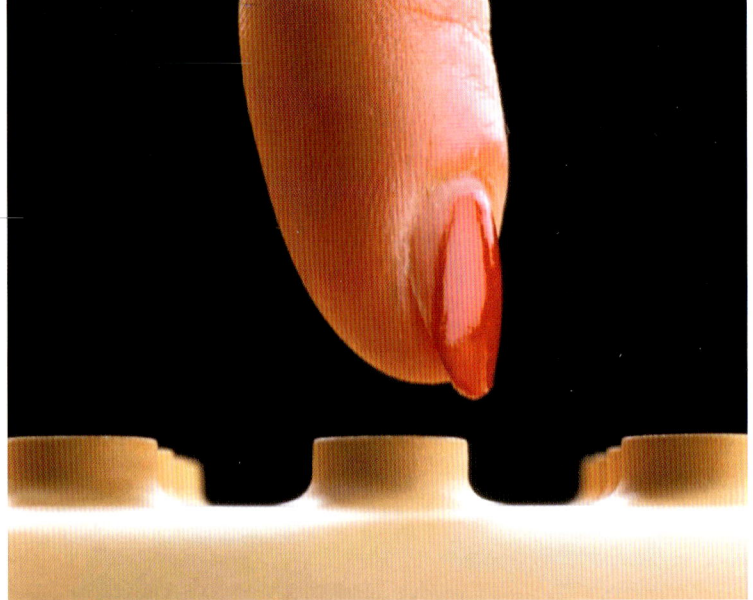

sketches, they do scale models, and they do tentatives, which is normal. It's really a process of doing, of making, of creating. Sometimes you've got an intuition, which is very rapid, and sometimes you have to verify what you are thinking. I call it a kind of Darwinian process, from one tentative to the other, a kind of trial and error. You do it and you change and then you do it and you change, and then you change and finally, you've got it.

CB Adriano Olivetti once said "design is a question of substance, not just form". Olivetti was a pioneer in demonstrating its understanding of what design could bring to a company. Was it this holistic approach that attracted you to Olivetti? How did it work in practice?

MB I was presented to Mr Olivetti, the son of Adriano, by a man who knew me for a couple of years, when I started experimenting and designing things. And he told him, listen Roberto, there is a young boy here who looks to be very, very gifted. Would you like to see him? He said yes. I went there, we talked for 30 minutes and he said okay you are my consultant for the new electronic era. That was the fact. But, of course, we all knew that there was a prestigious glare around Olivetti, and for me it was such an unbelievable opportunity, such a privilege, to start working with them.

And so, about form and substance ... what Adriano Olivetti said was terribly true, but it's obvious. Because a substance without form cannot exist, and vice versa.

CB But isn't the substance also connected to what their products meant to people, not just their form, but what their advertising strategy, and their image conveyed?

MB Of course. There are many, many levels at which the words substance and form can be evaluated. For example, after designing for Olivetti, for me, the real substance was this dramatic change from the electromechanical era towards the digital and electronic one. That was not only a technological change, it was a substance change, a substantial change.

And very, very fast all the office workers had to understand and perceive their office environments. Today the office is a table and a chair and a human. And the table is not necessarily your table, you know, the hot desk theory? You sit there with your laptop and that's your table. And then you close the laptop, you go out, and when you come back you can sit at another desk. Because everything now is in the cloud, yes?

CB Yes.

MB And you can talk to machines, you can change everything with your hands or with your voice, and we will very quickly go back to the origins of what started being called office work, which was all centred around humans, around his brain, around his will, around his activities. And that's the substance.

CB When I look at the Lettera 35 from 1974 I see a study in carefully controlled

The lectern form in Bellini's work, seen here in the Yamaha TC800D stereo cassette deck.

form through plane, line and curve which echoes earlier treatments to Olivetti typewriter casings. Yet it clearly demonstrates your interpretation of an existing form. To what extent were your designs observations on the past and formulations on the future?

MB To tell you the truth, that machine, being one of the few surviving ones still related to the mechanical structure, didn't inspire me so much. What you correctly see there, and you describe now, is a machine which follows the mainstream of those machines already designed. Of course, I tried to do it as much as I could, putting my hands on it, but you feel it as continuing a kind of slow way to design.

But that's limited to that machine. If you take my very innovative machines, like, I don't know, the Divisumma 18 or Logos 50/60 or the TCV 250, the one with the big eye. Or the ETP 55, the last electronic typewriter before they disappeared. All those were strongly innovative, and they make no reference to the past machines. It was impossible, because I was giving form to a new era. So I can answer yes and no. When I design a chair, for example, then your question is perfectly right.

And I will tell you that a chair is a chair is a chair. My very fortunate chair I designed 37 years ago for Cassina. It is the leather Cab chair. That it looks so similar to an ancient Egyptian chair is something I discovered by visiting a museum. And so I pay a lot of respect and attention to the continuity of form and images, because that is the continuity of the substance as well. It's a human sitting on something, you know?

But when the substance changes, and you go from electromechanical tools to the new totally free electronic ... if you consider today's electronics, there are no more comparisons with what was electronic 20 years or 30 years ago. For example, what satisfaction when television sets disappeared, becoming an image on a wall with just two dimensions. That, for me as a designer, is absolutely amazing. In that case you break the continuity, and you jump into another dimension.

CB One of the relationships *Interface* examines is the interplay between the arts and product design — for example Nizzoli's designs and mid-century modern forms by Henry Moore. To some extent these art forms inform each other. Can you talk about your experiences relative to this idea?

MB Yes, as a designer and as an architect, I understand. Artists influence each other and their work is an expression of their times. Meanwhile they contribute to and interpret their times. So if you are an artist, you belong to that flow of artistic experience, which represents, interprets and communicates our times. Absolutely, yes.

Your question, I feel, makes sense. But not in a deliberate way. If you are a true artist, you cannot be out of this flow of experience. Of course, now the landscape with art is getting much more complex. Once you could say Renaissance, Baroque, and so on, but today ... you've got an artist (Lucio Fontana) cutting the canvas,

"A chair is a chair is a chair".
Bellini's leather Cab chair for Cassina, 1977.

and revolutionising and changing the way to look at paintings, and then you've got another artist (Piero Manzoni) putting a shit in a can and saying this is art, and in fact, it is art.

And so, there is no one art, one style, one way of interpreting our times, which are getting more and more complex and rich and diversified. But the question you put is a good question, and I say yes, I feel myself as part of this process.

CB The mid 1960s saw an explosion of consumerism and mass culture reverberate in the work of American sculptor Claus Oldenburg and other pop artists, and we look at your Divisumma 18 and the Valentine typewriter, and the posters that were coming from Olivetti …

MB Of course the graphic design of Olivetti at the time, it was also part of this process. We didn't talk together so much, but we were interpreting and living our times. For example, the Divi 18, yes, it could be a little bit pop. It's the first time I hear somebody making that point. That's a good situation. But on the other side, I was trying to transform that machine, which was a hand machine, as a kind of grasp, like a piece of our body, you know?

CB Yes.

MB And to make it friendly to our hands, to make it as a little animal, talking to you, telling you something and being gentle. On the other hand it was a big advancement, because that integrated keyboard, then with one material, is at the base of the way today's electronic flat keyboard works. I don't know if that is true for the very latest ones, but it was for years.

CB When embarking on the design of the ImageWriter II printer, Apple designer Stephen Peart is quoted as saying "I asked myself, what would Bellini do?" How would you describe your influence on information technology design products and what aspects of your work in this area would you like to be most remembered for?

MB I am flattered by what Stephen said but I don't think much of my influence in that.

CB Oh no?

MB It is inclined, a slope, yes, but it has got a totally different attitude. It doesn't fly the same way my machine used to fly. It's more strong blocks, you know, but in a way, yes, I might have influenced it. The way I perceive I might have influenced that field is that I never felt myself as designing a case for new machines, but really to design machines, tools.

And I had the chance to invent new machines because I came in that very particular change of eras where I have set the new kind of animals, not existing before, starting anew from a human, a chair and a table, and not from a mechanism. And I never accepted to be guided by a mechanism, and I always tried to transform a mechanism into a machine.

A mechanism is something rough, which works on itself, all naked, put on a table with wires and levers and so on ... and a machine is something which has been domesticated by us, as humans, and transformed into something which has got part of us inside, because when a machine is domesticated, it's part of a human.

This is what I could have left with my design experience.

CB But I do see contemporary designers who strive to make technological products playful, they want you to discover how it works intuitively, instead of having to read the manual. Your work is part of the genesis of this playful and discovering nature, the encounter with the object that's still practised today.

MB Yes, that's well said. I didn't think about that, but what you are saying is convincing ... yes, it might be right. Me too, I hate manuals, for example.

CB Yes, don't we all.

MB And I'm always fighting with new machines which enter in your hands, or within your environment, and you have to fight to understand how it could work. And I hate reading manuals. And in fact there is more and more of this attitude of making machines self-understandable, teaching you how to work with them. And I think the Apple attitude has been towards that.

CB I also see a lack of interaction now, where you have a gesture interface and everything defers to a flat plane which you swipe your fingers across and there's no sound, no texture. It doesn't seem playful to me any more. Is this a dead end we've come to?

MB Yes, those things are going to become more and more immaterial. We will enter a more and more abstract world, when you might think something, and that will happen, or barely say a few words and that will happen. But in a way, that will also possibly become playful. For example, those games where you can simulate playing tennis, you know, against a screen, that's possibly another way to be playful. Of course we are going towards a rather scary world.

CB I agree. Mr. Bellini, thank you very much for speaking with me.

MB It's been a pleasure, because I must say, you have put very fundamental questions. The questions I found very interesting and close to myself.

THE THINKING MAN'S FOOD PROCESSOR

DOMESTICITY GENDER AND THE APPLE II

BY JESSE ADAMS STEIN [1]

IN ITS SHORT HISTORY THE PERSONAL COMPUTER TRANSITIONED FROM A HOBBYIST'S MACHINE INTO A CONSUMER APPLIANCE THAT GRADUALLY COLONISED THE FAMILY HOME. THIS ESSAY CONSIDERS THE THINKING BEHIND THE GROUND-BREAKING DESIGN AND MARKETING OF THE APPLE II PERSONAL COMPUTER AND ITS INFLUENCE ON SOCIAL ATTITUDES AND GENDER ROLES.

This 1960s image for IBM computers shows the gender stereotypes of the era: man at the controls, woman at the keyboard.

In the media-saturated beginnings of the 21st century it is easy to forget that not so long ago the personal computer had a contested identity in the collective imagination. The industrial design of the personal computer was not a 'natural' technological evolution: it was entangled with issues of gender, power, economics, and even domesticity. In its short history, the personal computer transitioned from a machine into an appliance, gradually colonising the whole house: living rooms, kitchens, home offices, and beds[2]. While popular commentaries often emphasise Apple products' beauty and desirability, this analysis moves away from questions of style or 'good design'. This essay considers the communicated messages manifest within the industrial design and marketing of the personal computer.

To clarify, the term 'personal computer' refers to devices that were first commercially marketed in the mid-1970s — microcomputer units designed for individual use (not to be confused with the other type of computer in use in the mid-20th century: room-sized data-processors). In designing and marketing personal computers, Apple – alongside corporations such as Commodore and IBM — had to manage existing social anxieties about the uptake of new technologies, for example, taking into account prejudiced assumptions about the connection between typing, keyboards, and 'women's work'. Notwithstanding the impact of feminism, social attitudes to gender roles in the home and the workplace were still fraught with tension and often highly inequitable[3].

In April 1977 Apple launched the first personal computer aimed at a mainstream consumer market, a wedge-shaped device called the Apple II, a microcomputer that users plugged into their television monitors[4]. The product was a commercial success. By 1978 Apple claimed to be the producer of the 'world's best-selling computer'[5]. A crucial part of the Apple II's success was its industrial design, which attempted to bestow upon the computer the identity of a reliable home appliance. Until the launch of Apple II, the microcomputer market was the domain of a subculture of hobbyists. Made up of a confusing array of exposed circuit-boards, microchips and wires, the hobbyist's machine lived in garages and basements and was interpretable only to a small group of zealous computer engineers and enthusiasts. The Apple II moved from the garage into the heart

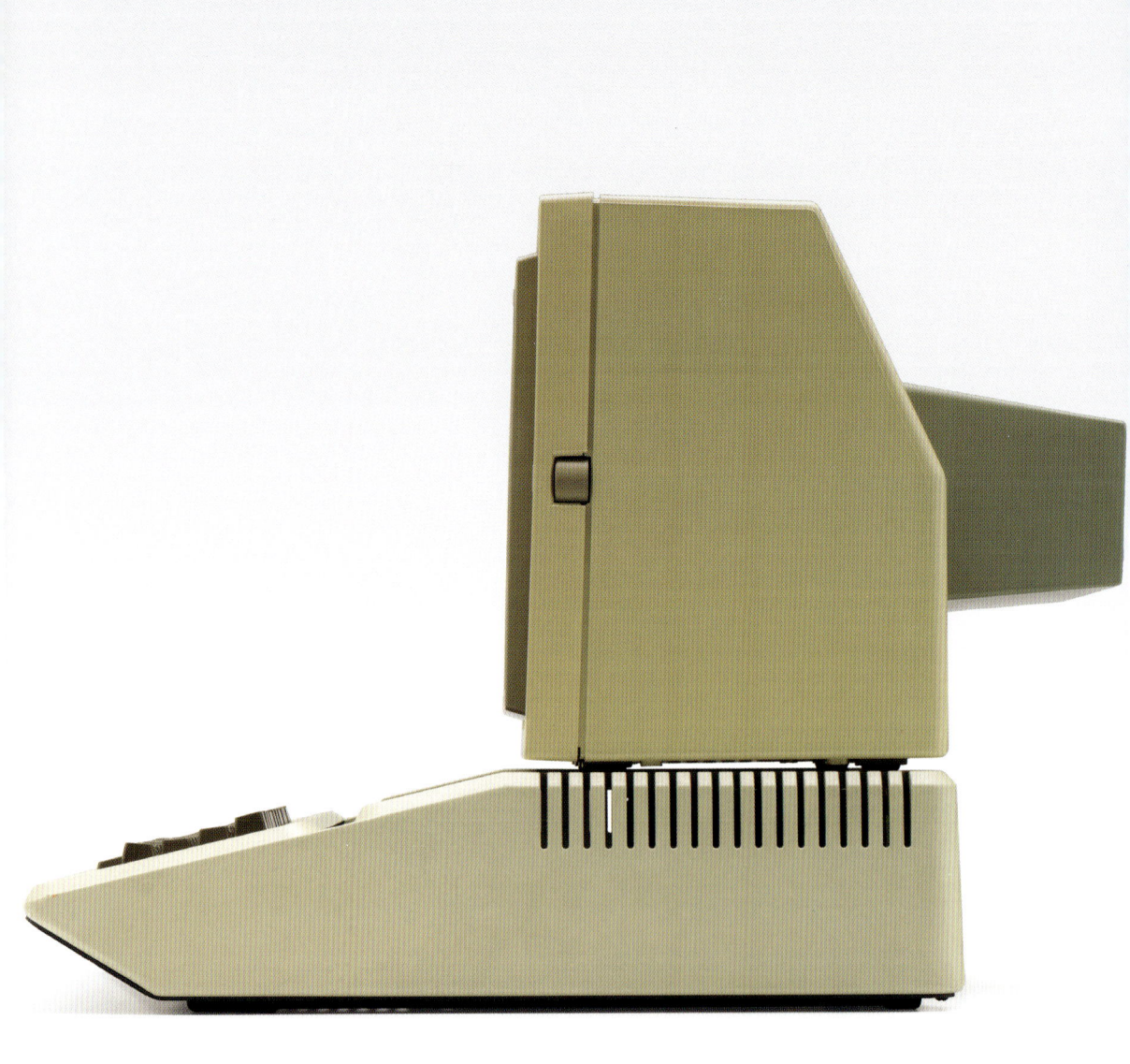

The simple reassuring design of the Apple II resembled a domestic appliance. It was originally sold without the monitor, which was not introduced until 1982.

of the house; and Apple shifted microcomputing from a small subculture into the mainstream.

With the introduction of the personal computer the home also became more like an office. It blurred the distinction between labour and leisure, and brought corporate culture into the home[6].

The industrial design of early personal computers has been connected to the visual language of space exploration, science fiction and popular cinema[7]. But the role that domesticity played in Apple Computer's design strategy in the 1970s and 1980s deserves further exploration, in terms of both industrial design and marketing. By connecting the world of computing with the domestic sphere, Apple produced a line of personal computer devices that communicated modernist values of efficiency, order, and stability. While the industrial design of other PC manufacturers of the late 1970s and 1980s presents a patchy lineage back to IBM's giant data-processors (as expressed in the use of primary colours, hard corners, and box-like forms[8]), Apple's early computer cases echo the simple, assuring, and hermetically-sealed plastic shells of 1970s domestic appliances. How did this happen?

DESIGNING THE APPLE II

In 1974 the computer engineer Steve Wozniak built the Apple I personal computer, and in 1976 Wozniak and his entrepreneurial friend Steve Jobs presented it for sale to computer enthusiasts at the Homebrew Computer Club in California[9]. The Apple I was a computer motherboard kit without a case — owners generally made their own. The machine catered to hobbyists who were eager to find uses for the newly released Intel microprocessor.

Although Apple I sales had been good within its limited market, Jobs envisioned that the personal computer could be sold to mainstream consumers, a market that did not exist at the time[10]. Technology commentator Leander Kahney suggests that Jobs "disliked [the] amateurish hobbyist aesthetic" of the Apple I and aimed to market a "straight-out-of-the-box" personal computer with broad appeal[11]. To break into this market, Jobs believed the next Apple computer – the Apple II – had to look like a consumable, it needed to inspire confidence in the face of mystifying computer functions[12]. This, Jobs decided, required one thing: plastic[13]. By early 1977, several small computing companies had begun creating personal computers using the new Intel technology, but virtually none had chosen to seal their units within manufactured plastic cases[14].

By 1976 Wozniak and Jobs had little money to launch into large-scale manufacturing of motherboards, let alone plastic cases. Nonetheless, Jobs managed to convince the out-of-work product designer Jerry Manock[15] to create a simple design for the Apple II case[16]. The need for speedy production was to prepare 20 Apple II computers for the West Coast Computer Faire in San Francisco in April 1977.

Several Apple commentators claim that Jobs hunted for design ideas for the Apple II case by wandering through the kitchen appliance section of department store Macy's examining the plastic forms encasing electric mixers and food processors[17]. One product that particularly appealed was the Cuisinart electric mixer, which Jobs allegedly used as an example when instructing Manock for the Apple II's design[18]. These appliances expressed the same principles of domestic comfort, stability, and efficiency that Jobs wanted in his first consumer-appliance microcomputer.

The resultant Apple II is encased in an angular beige shell, produced from two simple plastic components. It has a sloping wedge at the front, presenting an open face containing an in-built keyboard. The sides have vertical vents wrapping around the edges, and chamfered, 'grippable' corners[19]. To us today, it seems a large and graceless irregular prism. Manock's work for the Apple II is hardly an elegant design; it echoes the then-familiar chiselled and angular casings of calculators and kitchen appliances of the 1970s.

Apple II's case concealed the internal mechanics, obscuring the nature of data-processing. Users no longer needed to understand how a computer functioned when using the device. Thus a certain mystification took place — for both hobbyists and mainstream consumers. No longer could hobbyists pull apart their device and rewire it (lest they lose their warranty), and the 'mainstream consumer' never fully understood the workings of the computer. The plastic case became what they understood the word computer to mean.

The 1977 advertisement for the Apple II moves the computer into the domestic setting and introduces a subtle shift in gender roles.

At the time of its release, the Apple II's form appeared to be utilitarian and functional. The warm hum of the self-contained Apple II, the dull clack of its brown keys, the comforting tactility of its bevelled edges and chamfered corners conveys a sense of assurance, even as users attempted complex programming.

MARKETING THE APPLE II

Using the Apple II could be a frustrating process that required patience, and the constant presence of the Apple BASIC manual of commands. Consequently, Apple's early marketing strategy emphasised simplicity, comfort and reassurance. In the early years, Apple's advertising and marketing was handled by the Regis McKenna agency.

Consider the Apple II Introduction, a full-page advertisement that first appeared in the July 1977 issue of *Byte* magazine[20]. The Apple II computer is presented in a fashionable 1970s kitchen, sitting atop a wooden table, adjacent to a man in a blue skivvy. Let's call him Bob. Bob's Apple II is accompanied by a monitor (possibly a television), and a pile of papers[21]. The apparent 'normality' of this scene is reinforced by the woman, in soft-focus, in the kitchen background: let's call her Norma. To Norma's right is an appliance that looks remarkably like a Cuisinart electric mixer — the appliance that is said to have inspired Jobs at Macy's.

The choice of the kitchen for Apple II's introduction is significant. Although still more or less coded as a female domain, the 1970s American kitchen also inferred ideas of efficient productivity, and was understood as an informal social setting in the popular image of the middle-class American home. This conscious informality tipped the Apple II as the thinking man's food processor.

The Apple II Introduction tells us much about Apple's careful negotiation of existing gender stereotypes, and about how Apple encouraged the emergence of men as computer consumers. The parallels between Bob and Norma — and the Apple II and the electric mixer — are hardly subtle. The familiarity of the domestic scene — including its warm colours and the smiling approval of a woman — makes this image of domestic microcomputing appear safe for an apprehensive public.

Why do we need Norma's approving smile? Let us recall the historical context. Juliet Webster reminds us that: "In the days of the typewriter, the photocopier, and the filing cabinet (highly gendered technologies from which men kept their distance) … men fostered their own ignorance of these technologies in order to successfully maintain this distance, eschewing, for instance, the operation of keyboards, lest they be seen to be performing a 'low grade' function."[22]

The tools that women used to enable their work — such as the typewriter — were correspondingly feminised. And so it was that the keyboard, regardless of whether it was attached to a computer or a typewriter, continued to carry an emasculating threat. Companies such as Apple needed to gently encourage and normalise computer use for male consumers.

In much of Apple's advertising and manual material up to 1983[23], men are rarely presented typing[24]. They are frequently depicted as managers, overlooking others working on the computer, or, if they are sitting directly at the computer, they tend to only have one hand on the keyboard, while the other hand engages in an action, such as holding a drink. Accordingly we can see how the Apple II Introduction reinforced ideas about masculinity through the cultivation of distance between Bob and the keyboard. Norma's assuring smile indicates that she endorses Bob's activity. Bob's left hand rests possessively on the keyboard. This, and the graphs on the computer monitor, tells us that he is not passively typing. He is entering commands.

The Apple II Introduction presents the promise of Bob's control over his various domains — at home, and in business. Bob's graph-generating program answers the question, 'What am I worth?' The images that surround him, his so-called possessions — his house, his wife, his technology — further enforce that sense of control. Thus the spheres of domesticity, labour, commercial interest, and ownership overlap, and the distinctions between work and leisure, and between pleasure and control are muddled. The Apple II is an active artefact at the centre of this network.

FAN FRICTION

DESIGN-CENTRIC BATTLE LINES IN THE SMART PHONE AGE

BY SEAMUS BYRNE

IN THE DESIGN-CONSCIOUS CONSUMER TECHNOLOGY MARKET, BRAND LOYALTY HAS NEVER BEEN MORE PASSIONATE. CONSUMERS ARE OFTEN DIVIDED INTO THOSE WHO VALUE DESIGN OVER SPECIFICATIONS AND FEATURES AND THOSE WHO DON'T. THIS ESSAY EXAMINES THE STYLE VERSUS SUBSTANCE DEBATE AROUND SMART PHONES AND CONCLUDES THAT THE ISSUE IS NEITHER SIMPLE NOR CLEAR CUT.

The devices are an extension of us. We would rather lose our wallets than our smart phones.

Marc Newson, world-renowned Australian industrial designer, was asked why there is such passionate disagreement around whether an iPhone is worth its price. Even someone of his stature in the design world found it simplest to declare "people just get it or they don't"[1]. Thus the battle lines of fandom are born, where specifications and features are considered worthy of debate while ephemeral notions of design — of materials, engineering tolerances, finishes and so on — are dismissed as window dressing. In the same Q&A discussion Newson explains that "the better something is made, the less noise it makes. The less people understand. The simpler something is, the more complex it is."[1]

In the modern era, the design-focused approach to consumer technology, led by Apple's Steve Jobs, has been a clarion call or a red rag, depending on your perspective. Apple has always been marked by an 'us and them' divide, by its own intent, even when it only made personal computers. In those earlier times Apple versus Microsoft was once described as a Catholic versus Protestant divide by Umberto Eco [2].

From Apple's '1984' advertisement painting itself as a destroyer of digital monotony to its Think Different campaign aligning itself with "The misfits. The rebels. The troublemakers.", Apple has relished its status as the 'other'. As that Think Different campaign proclaimed: "You can praise them, disagree with them, quote them, disbelieve them, glorify or vilify them. About the only thing you can't do is ignore them."[3]

Since the launch of the iPhone and Apple's rise from challenger to the industry's dominant force, glorification and vilification have been delivered in generous measure. The fervour itself, for and against certain products and brands, has never been more passionate than in this era when the devices in question are an extension of us. We carry them everywhere. We would rather lose our wallets than our phones. When we are alone in this world today we turn our attention to that glowing screen that brings the world to us. What are these products if not companions that we want to fall in love with?

Some, including industry leaders, argue that the latest communication technology devices rightly need to elevate style over substance. In September 2011, Blackberry's UK Managing Director, Stephen Bates, told *T3* magazine:

"Smart phones have become like a fashion accessory. It matters what they look like, it matters what brand they are, it matters what the look and feel is so that you can not only have a very functionally usable device, but you have something you can be proud of."[4]

In October of the same year Samsung UK's Sales Director, Andrew Glass, also spoke to *T3*. "Style is often more important than substance to smart phone consumers. It's definitely a part of the buying decision, I think style is certainly big on the agenda for most people buying mobiles now."[5]

But style is not simple a question of fashion. Nokia successfully brought fashion to mobile phones in the 1990s with the introduction of swappable covers on its wildly popular handsets. Fashion is a surface layer while good design touches everything. Stephen Fry, an avowed aesthete and gadget lover, sums up the design lover's view of why style really matters.

"As if style and substance are at war! As if a device can function if it has no style. As if a device can be called stylish that does not function superbly ... Fiddly buttons, blocky icons, sickeningly stupid nested menus — these are the enemy. They waste time, militate against function and lower the spirits. They make the user feel frustrated and (quite wrongly) dense ... So, yes, beauty matters. Boy, does it matter. It is not surface, it is not an extra, it is the thing itself."[6]

While Fry decries the idea of style and substance being at war, this is the war in question. Design lovers see the interplay of deeply integrated, high quality design as a critical part of the final product performance. Critics see style as a distraction

from the real engineering marvels of CPU, RAM, storage, screen size, resolution and other numerically quantifiable features.

After Apple redefined smart phone technology with the iPhone in 2007, the arrival of its key competitor, Google's Android operating system, delivered a technology face-off unlike any other in the history of consumer devices. Android arrived as the open source yin to the Apple's highly controlled yang, available to a wide range of hardware makers so that a quality smart phone experience would compete on price and performance.

Today, Android is the dominant operating system in the mobile landscape, spread across thousands of devices and brands across the globe. It is like the Windows PC of the mobile world. But when it comes to singular devices there is still nothing that compares to Apple and its iPhone.

The Apple '1984' marketing campaign positioned the company as the destroyer of digital monotony.

To Android lovers, they make their choice based on the extra freedoms and extensions available to them that Apple does not provide. Apple makes smart phones that have fixed batteries, no memory expansion options, proprietary charging and synchronisation connectors and small screen sizes. Any one of these individual factors could be the one that tips the balance in favour of Android.

To Apple fans, what Apple leaves out is precisely what makes its products so good. A fixed battery and no memory expansion mean a design that doesn't have to accommodate opening panels or expose internal hardware. It leads to thinner finished products. The smaller screen size is part of Apple's focused vision on a one-handed smart phone experience.

After the launch of the original Apple Macintosh computer, Steve Jobs said in a 1985 *Playboy* interview: "When you're a carpenter making a beautiful chest of drawers, you're not going to use a piece of plywood on the back, even though it faces the wall and nobody will ever see it. You'll know it's there, so you're going to use a beautiful piece of wood on the back. For you to sleep well at night, the aesthetic, the quality, has to be carried all the way through."[7]

This is where we find the same objective details can result in very different subjective feelings from advocates and critics. Where one sees perfection another sees extravagance.

Apple's attitude to the iPhone cable connector has been a particular sore point. Where the wider industry supports the USB standard, Apple has consistently used its own cable technologies. In 2012 Apple introduced a thin 'Lightning' connector that, for the first time, allowed the cable to be inserted in any orientation.

John Gruber, professional designer and notable Apple commentator, points out this demonstrates the divide perfectly: "The Lightning adapter epitomises what makes Apple Apple. To the company's fans, it provides elegance and convenience —

The first generation Apple iPhone 2G, launched in 2007.

it's just so much nicer than micro-USB. To the company's detractors, it exists to sell $29 proprietary adapters and to further enable Apple's fetish for device thinness. Neither side is wrong."[8]

For some it should never be about anything other than what a device can do for the price. If you have to pay more for a device because its chassis has been etched from a single block of aluminium then you're paying extra for the wrong thing. For others this is exactly the kind of design choice they want to carry each day and are willing to pay for.

After each smart phone launch technology analysis firm IHS iSuppli does a cost breakdown of the device's actual parts. For the 16GB iPhone 5S its analysis showed a bill of materials cost of US$191 for an implied margin of 69% [9]. To define a product as the sum of its parts shows a preference for the tangible that plays direct counterpoint to those who would choose a device based on nothing but its appearance.

Yet the iSuppli report also recognises a range of features "that have never been seen before in a smart phone"[9]. A new 64-bit architecture, new radio frequency hardware, and a fingerprint scanner are all based on a great deal of engineering innovation that underpins Apple's reputation for delivering 'simple' solutions to complex problems.

At the other end of the spectrum the more design-loving buyer's first take on a new product is the unboxing video. Fans love to see the first impressions of those lucky enough to get their hands on new devices before the rest as they open up the box. How is it packaged? What extras are included? How does that first moment smell? It is as much about seeing what's in the box as seeing someone react for the first time.

Apple takes this seriously. The company employs a packaging designer who tests hundreds of box designs to ensure boxes open slowly. Not so slowly that it feels difficult, but just slowly enough to make that moment feel like a grand reveal [10].

To its fans, this is another reason to love Apple's passion for complete product design. while detractors argue that Apple charges too much money for products that only do the same or less than the competition. It is not wrong to make a choice based on personal preferences and ideals — choosing to denigrate those who chose differently is — but it is the hallmark of any deeply held fanaticism, whether religious, sporting or political.

More Android phones may be sold today than any other, but when it comes to single brand and single handset preferences it is the iPhone that continues to break opening weekend sales records each year.

When asked whether it was design that can be credited with the resurrection of Apple from its trouble in the 1990s, Newson responded: "The proof is there ... Design has played a big part in the reinvention of that brand. And it is now far and away the most valuable company in the world. Like an order of magnitude. And it's extraordinary. That's design."[11]

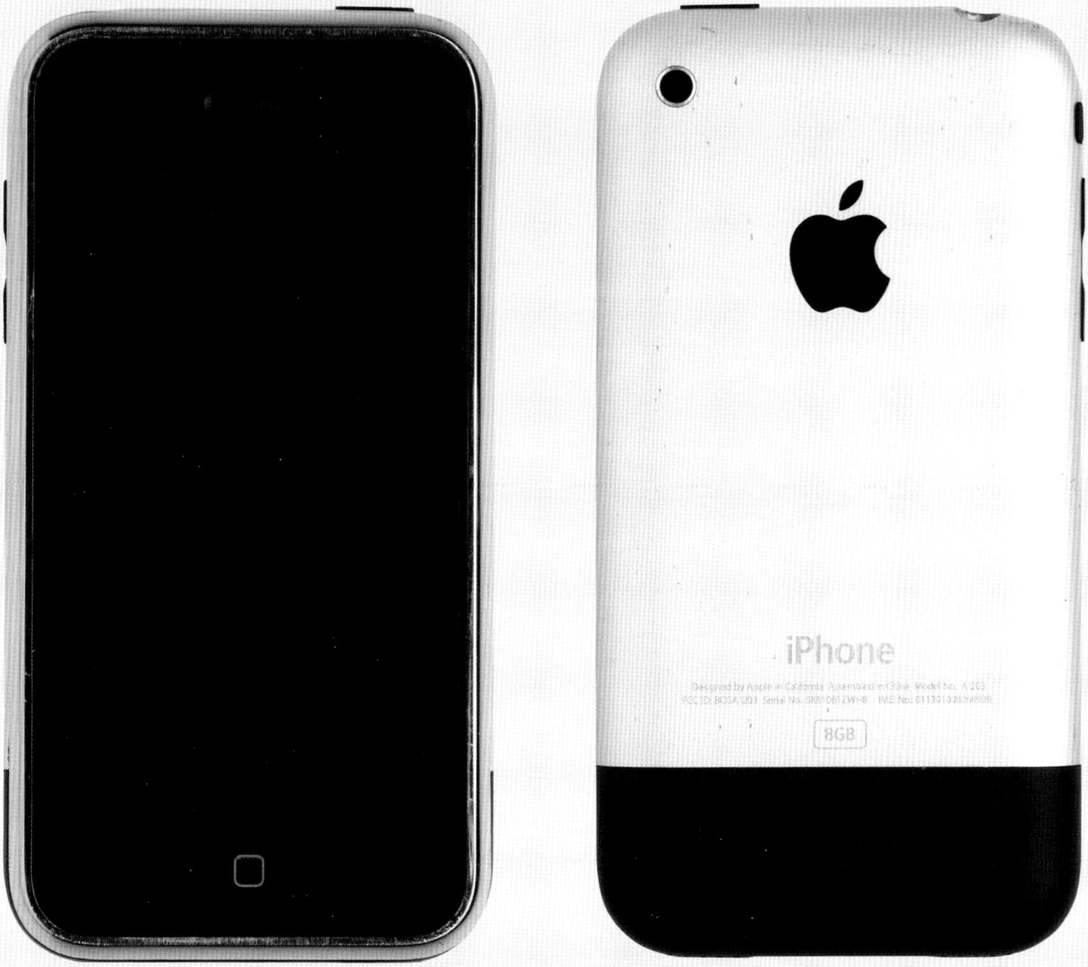
iPhone
8GB

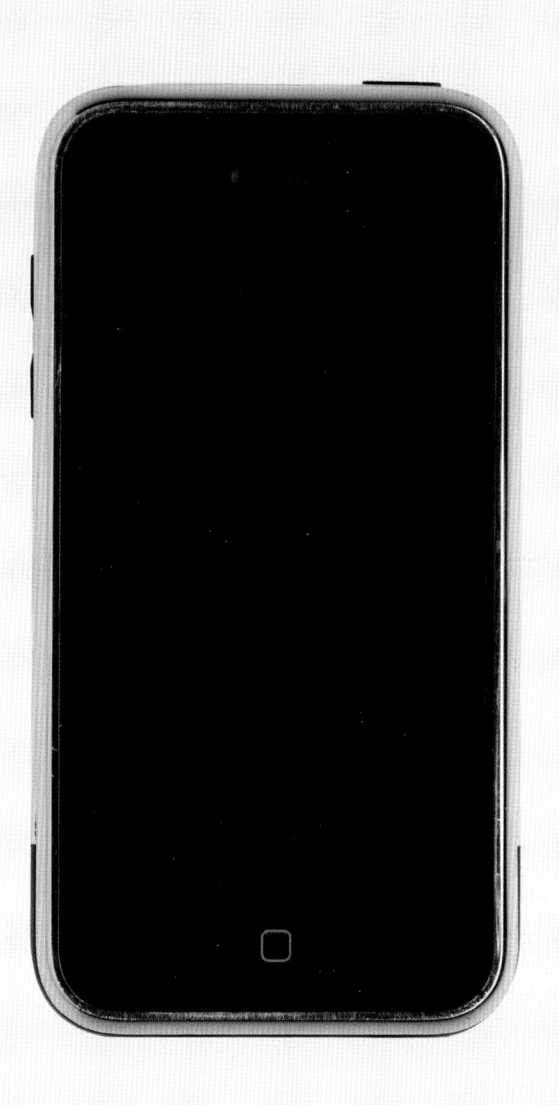

THE ENTHUSIASTS

WE SHAPE OUR TOOLS

ENTHUSIASTS OR EARLY ADOPTERS ENGAGE WITH A NEW TECHNOLOGY FOR ITS OWN SAKE, REGARDLESS OF HOW COMPLICATED OR IMPRACTICAL IT MAY BE. THIS SECTION INCLUDES OUTSTANDING EARLY EXAMPLES OF INFORMATION TECHNOLOGY DESIGN SUCH AS TYPEWRITERS, TELEPHONES, CALCULATORS, RADIOS AND PERSONAL COMPUTERS. THEY ILLUSTRATE HOW THE HUMAN-MACHINE INTERFACE GRADUALLY DEVELOPED; HOW DESIGNERS BEGAN TO SHAPE AND INFLUENCE EARLY TECHNOLOGY DEVICES; AND HOW PREFERRED ELEMENTS OF DESIGN BECAME THE NORM.

STUDIES IN DESIGN BOOK
Written by Christopher Dresser
Published by Gibbs Smith
England, 1874-1876
W: 305mm H: 430mm D: 40mm

British industrial designer Christopher Dresser (1834–1904) was a pioneer of a modern aesthetic that was radical at that time. An outspoken proponent of modern design, Dresser designed fabrics, metalwork and ceramics and his contributions to the understanding of new domestic product design in the industrial age were vast.

Dresser published a number of influential books throughout his career including this one about interior decoration. He wrote: "My book is intended to help the decorator and to enable those who live in decorated houses to judge, to an extent, the merit of the ornament around them."[1]

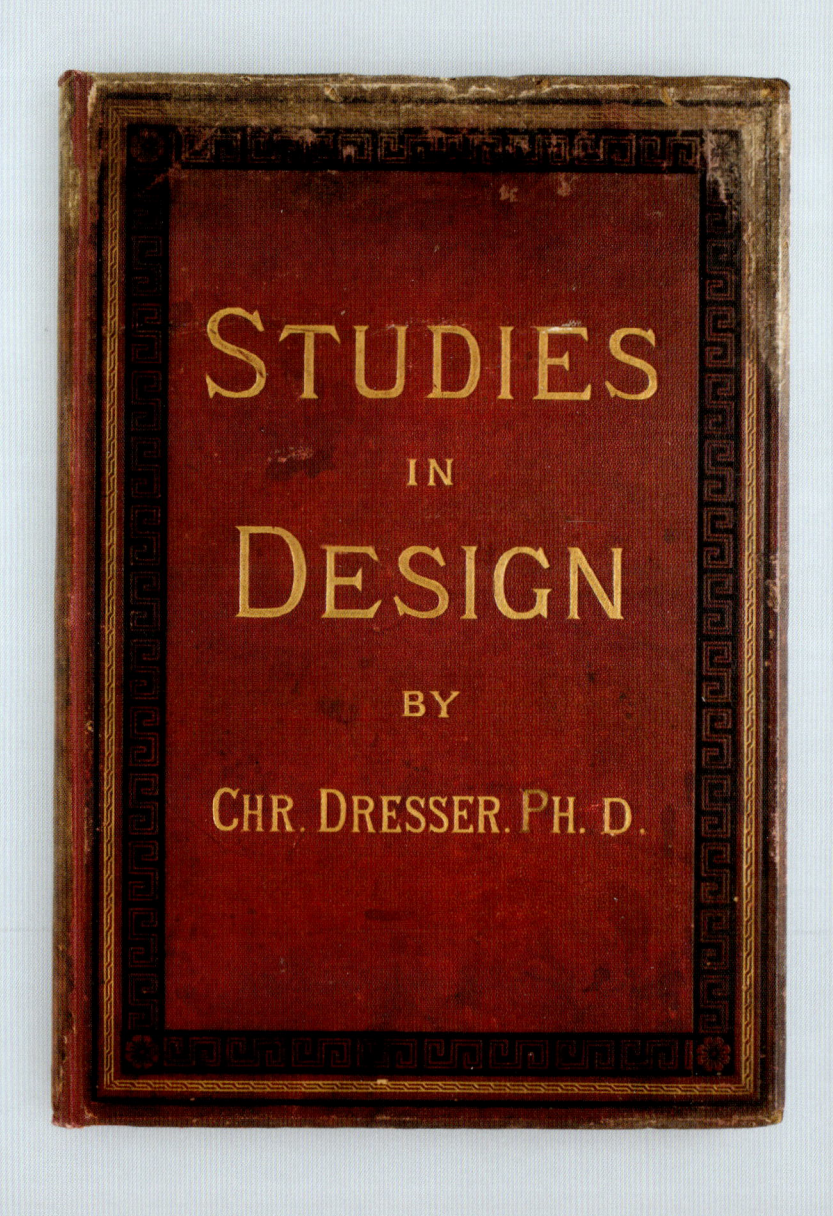

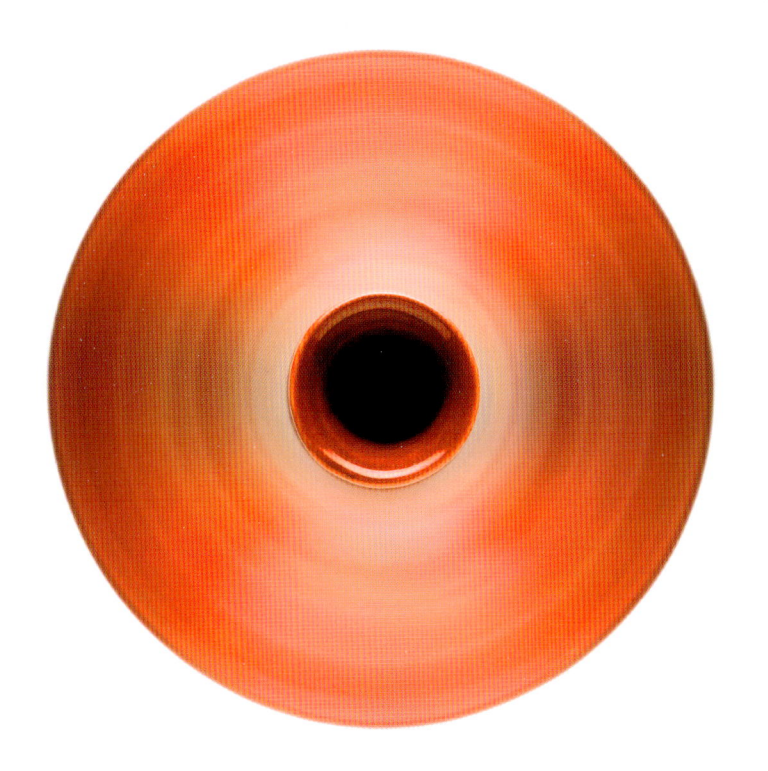

EARTHENWARE VASE
Designed by Christopher Dresser
Made by Linthorpe Pottery
England, about 1880
H: 186mm Dia: 186mm

Dresser was studious in his efforts to understand new techniques of production and, most importantly, reconsider artefacts from a viewpoint of use, manufacture and symbolic value.

He rejected the contemporary Victorian penchant for rich decoration. The restrained form and palette of this vase illustrates his innovative approach to a traditional object. Dresser was a fervent supporter of scientific progress and the new machine age. He associated simplicity with progress and this informed his economic use of materials.

EDMONDSONS PATENT
W.F. STANLEY
GREAT TURNSTILE
LONDON W.C.
A
B
C

MECHANICAL CALCULATOR
Designed by Joseph Edmonson
Made by W F Stanley
England, 1880
W: 495mm H: 120mm D: 415mm

Mechanical calculators were first developed to save time and reduce errors made by human calculators — an asset that was valued in any business or institution that required reliable calculations.

This circular calculating machine was patented by Joseph Edmonson in England in 1883. Used for addition and subtraction, Edmondson's circular calculator has a brass and steel mechanism housed in a wooden case. It was reliable and robust but it was a complex instrument to master. The operator had to know where and how to set the numbers to be used in the calculation, how to perform the function and where to read the result. These challenges created a barrier to its comprehension and operation.

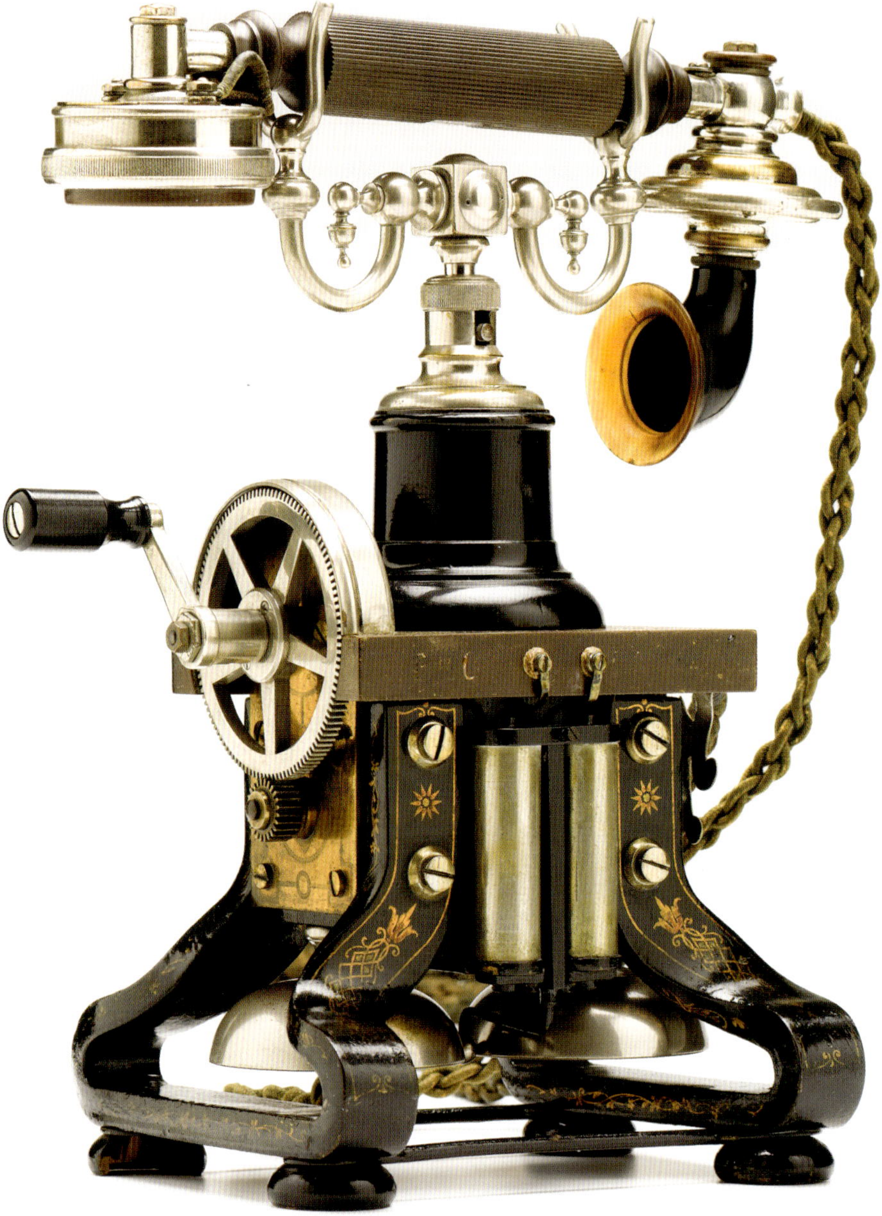

'EIFFEL TOWER' TABLE TOP TELEPHONE
Made by L M Ericsson
Sweden, 1892
W: 260mm H: 300mm D: 140mm

This was one of the first telephones to incorporate microphone and receiver elements into a single handset and one of the first free-standing telephones designed for a table top. Prior to this nearly all telephones were wall mounted.

A wall-mounted telephone was a convenient solution to concealing the circuit lines, which were safely contained in the wall cavity. However, it required the user to stand by the wall and speak into a fixed microphone while holding a receiver to their ear. The ability to sit down at a desk to take or make a call must have appealed to many established and new telephone users.

This telephone, known as the 'Eiffel Tower', presents a unique design with all the elements of the phone visible. The magneto (electrical generator that provided the ringing current), bells, wiring and handset are all mounted off the forged iron frame. It was popular and remained in production from 1892–1929, with sales of a million units over that period. The design was copied by several manufacturers.

**BLICKENSDERFER 6
PORTABLE TYPEWRITER**
Designed by George Canfield Blickensderfer
USA, 1906
W: 300mm H: 130mm D: 275mm

The Blickensderfer 6 was among the first truly portable typewriters. Many of the larger metal components were made of aluminium, which combined strength and lightness. The absence of any casing around the mechanism creates a skeletal form and gives the Blickensderfer a visual lightness.

George Blickensderfer (1850–1917) designed a cylindrical wheel with the characters embossed on it to replace the then commonly used mechanism with individual bars connected to the keys. This drastically reduced the number of parts required for the mechanism. All these elements combined to make the Blickensderfer lighter, smaller and cheaper than other typewriters, which helped its commercial success.

The typewriter had a full keyboard in the DHIATENSOR arrangement, originally designed by James Bartlett Hammond to avoid the problems of jamming. Blickensderfer's cylindrical wheel is similar to the golf ball mechanism later employed by IBM for the Selectric typewriter in 1961.

47

ELECTRIC KETTLE
Designed by Peter Behrens
Made by AEG
Germany, 1909
W: 255mm H: 350mm D: 280mm

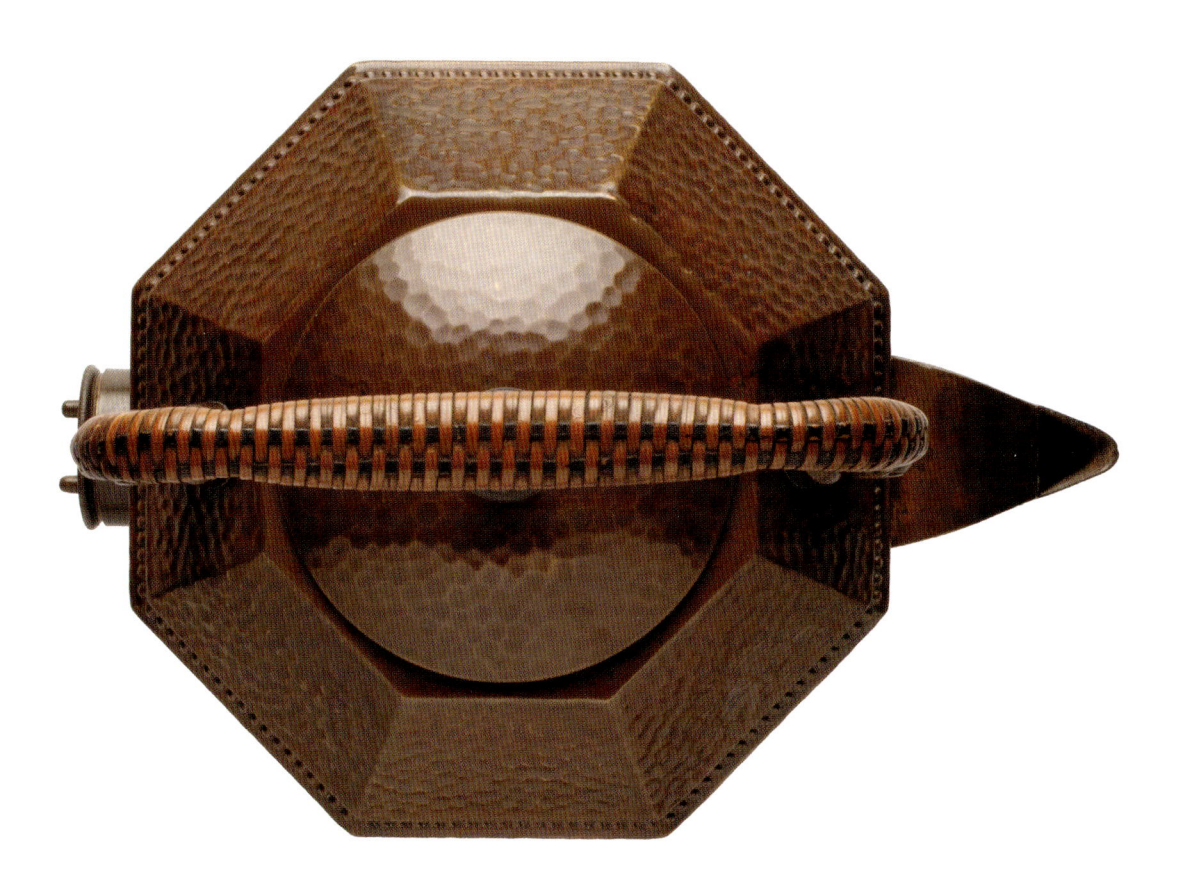

Peter Behrens (1868–1940) was a German architect and industrial designer. He designed this kettle for the German electrical equipment company AEG, which was founded in the 1880s. A range of permutations allowed the customer to select from different shapes, finishes and sizes to suit their needs. This was to be known and appreciated later as system design.

Behrens was part of a group of renowned German designers who established their reputations in the early years of the 20th century. Working together, Behrens and AEG helped bridge the gap between sophisticated mass production technology and a modern design strategy and vision. The influence of Behrens' design philosophy can be gauged by the people who worked in Behrens' studio in Neu-Babelsberg. They included Walter Gropius, Adolf Meyer, Ludwig Mies van der Rohe, Jean Cramer, Peter Grossman and Le Corbusier[2].

This page from a 1912 AEG price list for electric kettles shows the size and finish options available for the octagonal-shaped kettle. AEG also manufactured kettles in squat teardrop and cylindrical forms with the same size and finish options, demonstrating the application of Behrens' system design.

DIE FORM OHNE ORNAMENT BOOK
Published by Deutscher Werkbund (DWB)
Germany, 1924
W: 195mm H: 265mm D: 15mm

Die form ohne ornament (Form without ornament) was the first in the series *Bucher der form* (Books on form). The series contained critical essays and images of products that exemplified what the DWB considered examples of preeminent modern industrial design.

Counting Peter Behrens, Richard Riemerschmidt, Josef Maria Olbrich and Josef Hoffmann among its founding members, the DWB was an association of German architects, designers and industrialists who supported new forms that demonstrated an understanding of materials and technologies in mass production and considered ornament indulgent and unnecessary.

FIELD RADIO DEVICE (E 143A)
Designed and made by Telefunken
Germany, 1918
W: 370mm H: 250mm D: 128mm

This field radio was designed and manufactured by German company Telefunken in 1918. It is part of a larger field set used by the German military towards the end of World War I. Although this early radio was used by those trained in its intricacies (an enthusiast level of engagement was required) it had strong visual elements to guide them.

One of its most striking design elements is the early use of plastic in the dials arrayed across the face of the machine. The controls and switches are distinguished by various markings and shapes which cue the user as to their parameter, purpose and range of operation. When compared to English or French radio design from the same period, this consideration of the user demonstrates Telefunken's superior 'human factor' engineering. The prowess of Telefunken's physicists also quickly led the German company to the forefront of radio developments.

VOLKSEMPFÄNGER VE 301W RADIO
Designed by Otto Griessing and Walter Maria Kersting
Made by Lumophon, Bruckner & Stark
Germany, 1933
W: 280mm H: 392mm D: 175mm

This radio was developed by engineer Otto Griessing (1897–1958), and the Bakelite cabinet was designed by Walter Maria Kersting (1889–1970), the Professor of Artistic and Technical Design at the Cologne School of Design.

The Volksempfänger (People's receiver) radio was produced under a program initiated by German Minister for Propaganda Joseph Goebbels. Radio was a relatively new medium and radio receivers were prohibitively expensive at the time. Goebbels realised radio's potential to deliver Adolf Hitler's powerful oratories and the ability to control the reception and broadcast of information. His brief to engineer Griessing was to design and mass produce an affordable radio receiver for German citizens.

From 1933 to 1939 over nine million radio receivers were manufactured. They were built jointly by 28 manufacturers including AEG, Braun, Blaupunkt, Eumig, Loewe, Lorenz, Philips, Siemens and Telefunken among others. The Volksempfänger illustrates what a powerful tool radio was, and still is, to both inform and influence the community.

The number 301 in the model's title is a reference to 30 January 1933, the day after Hitler seized power in Germany.

ICO MP1 (MODELLO PORTATILE 1) TYPEWRITER

Designed by Aldo Magnelli and Riccardo Levi
Made by Olivetti
Italy, 1932
W: 300mm H: 135mm D: 340mm

The Ico (an acronym for Ingegnere Camillo Olivetti, the founder of Olivetti) was an enormously successful product, remaining in production from 1932 until 1950. It follows the template for the 'Olivetti style' set down by Camillo Olivetti in 1912: "a typewriter should not be a geegaw (a bauble or trinket) for the drawing room, ornate and in questionable taste. It should have an appearance that is elegant and serious at the same time."[3]

The influence of developments in modern art is apparent in Olivetti's design. Alberto Magnelli, the brother of case designer Aldo Magnelli, was an established painter who was involved in the abstract and concrete art movements. The form of the Ico typewriter casing, with semi circular curves around the type basket transitioning to perpendicular straight sides, is reminiscent of the vocabulary of forms employed by these artists.

Prior to joining Olivetti Magnelli had worked with Enrico Fermi in experimental physics. The Ico's mechanical design is by Riccardo Levi. Olivetti's product development structure was not hierarchical so engineering and design were equal partners and collaboration flourished.

This poster for the Ico was designed by Xanti Schawinsky in 1935. Schawinsky had studied at the Bauhaus in the mid 1920s. His skills were embraced by Olivetti in creating graphics that projected an image of a modern company.

55

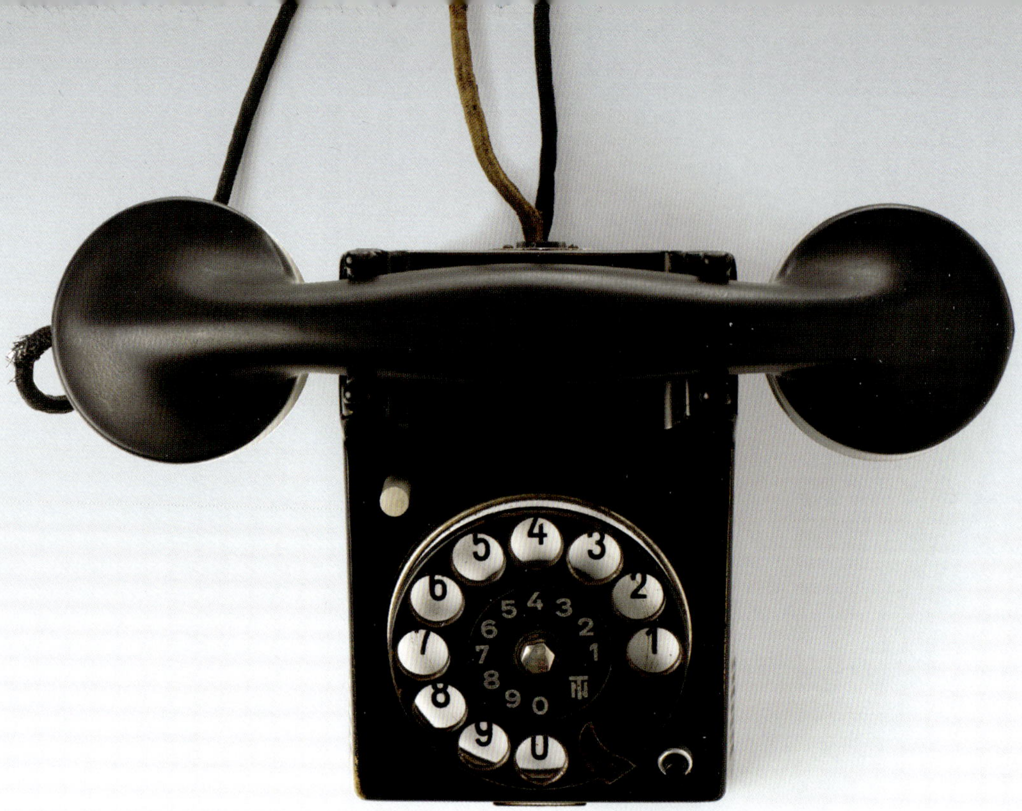

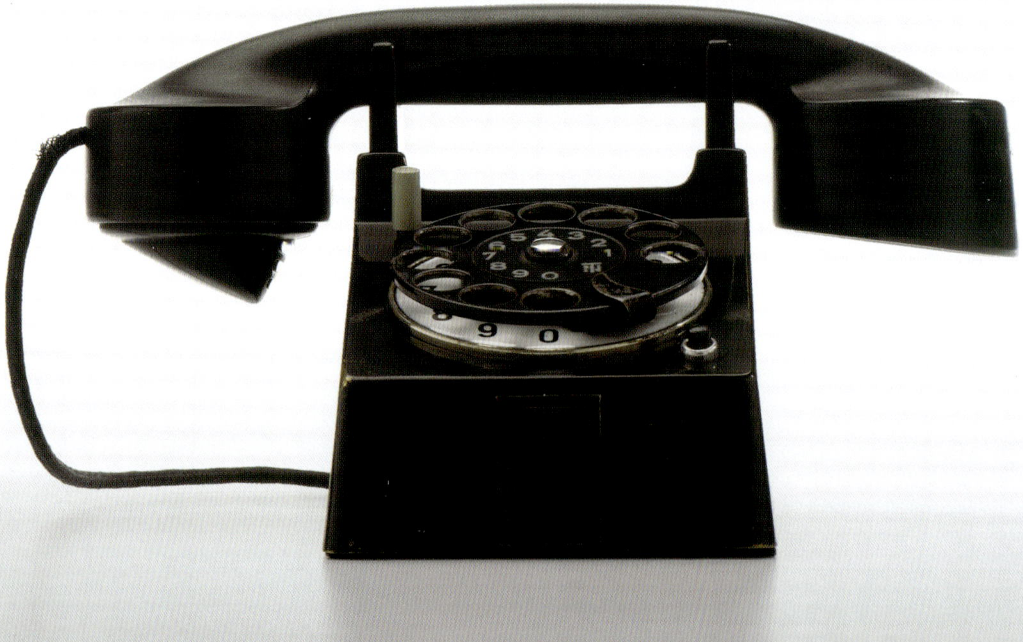

'BAUHAUS' TELEPHONE

Designed by Marcel Breuer and
Richard Schadewell
Made by Fuld & Co /
Telephonbau & Normazeit GmbH
Germany, 1928
W: 250mm H: 135mm D: 165mm

The design of this telephone has been attributed to Marcel Breuer (1902–81) who was engaged to design the new factory buildings for Fuld & Co in 1927–8. It was selected for the New Frankfurt housing program; a modern low cost development intended to relieve the post-World War I housing shortage. Every apartment was fitted with one of these phones, the parts of which were standardised and mostly made in small workshops. The Deutscher Werkbund and the Bauhaus were involved in the project, and so it is often called the Bauhaus phone.

The telephone design fulfils the modernist-functionalist criteria demanded by the project. Its form is an arresting departure from contemporary telephone design. It uses a mixture of materials, with the body in black lacquered sheet brass and a substantial bakelite handset extending significantly wider than the body. The rotary dial presents a strong design element, residing neatly in the middle of the square-faced base.

SUMMA 15 CALCULATOR
Designed by Marcello Nizzoli
Made by Olivetti
Italy, 1949
W: 255mm H: 150mm D: 350mm

Marcello Nizzoli designed this mechanical desktop calculator in collaboration with 'the mechanic' Natale Capellaro. The ergonomic design has resulted in a device that offers a fluid movement for the operator's hand in the performance of a function. After an amount is entered, the operator's hand moves toward the lever with the thumb setting the yellow joystick to the required operation as it passes. The lever is then pulled forward and released.

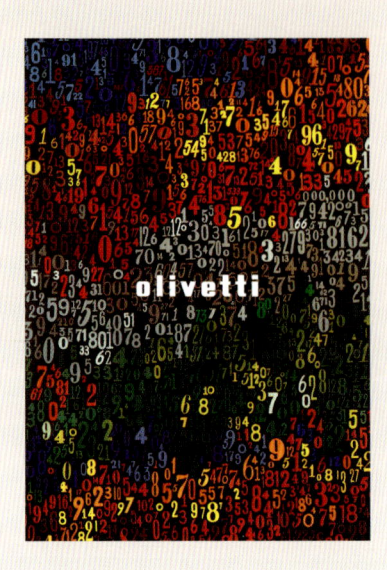

In 1936, the same year that Nizzoli became Olivetti's chief design consultant, artist and graphic designer Giovanni Pintori also joined Olivetti. Nizzoli and Pintori worked on architectural, product and publicity design. Olivetti posters project an image of the company and seldom focus on the purpose of its products. This poster by Pintori is composed of numeric characters, with the company name only emerging on closer inspection.

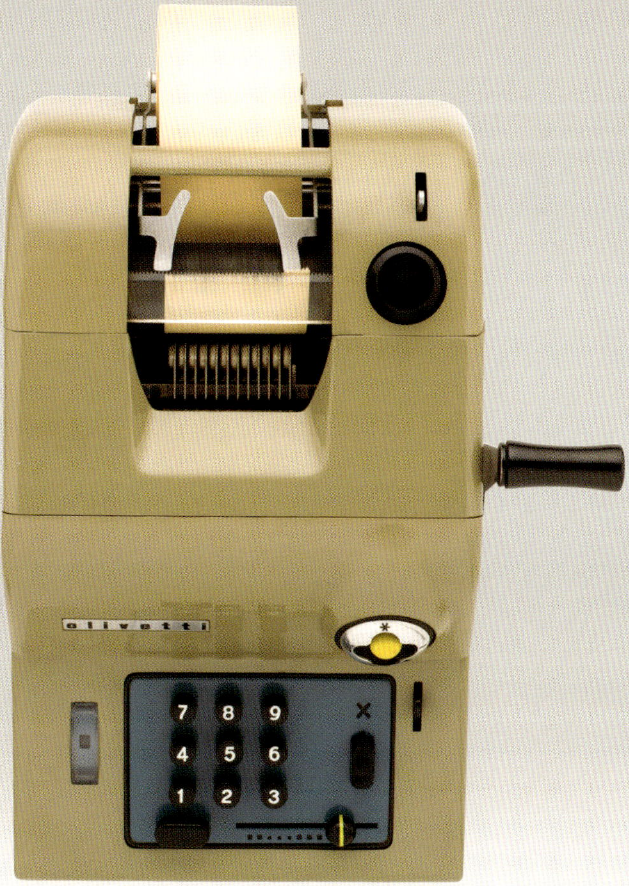
olivetti
7 8 9
4 5 6
1 2 3

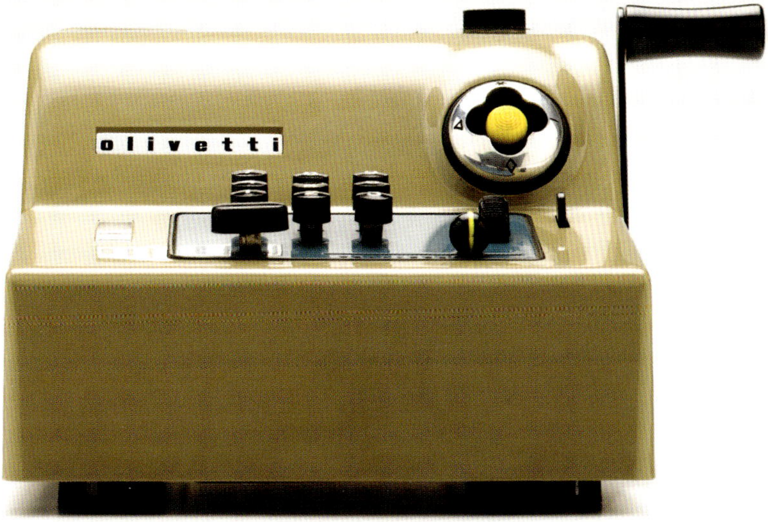
olivetti

LETTERA 22 TYPEWRITER
Designed by Marcello Nizzoli and
Giuseppe Beccio
Made by Olivetti
Italy, 1950
W: 270mm H: 80mm D: 320mm

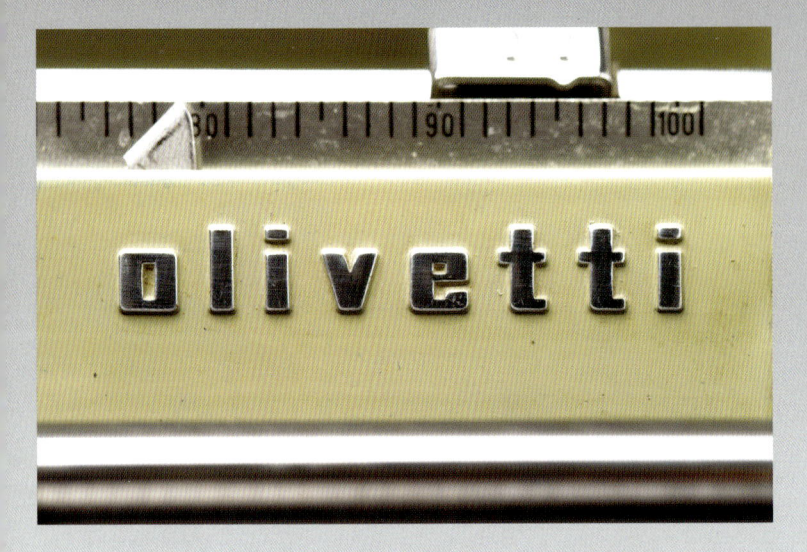

The Lettera 22 was the result of a collaboration between Marcello Nizzoli, one of Italy's finest industrial designers, and Giuseppe Beccio, who revolutionised the internal engineering of the machine. Beccio reduced the number of parts in the assembly from around 3000 to 2000. This shortened the assembly time, lowered the cost of production, and made the purchase of the Lettera 22 more competitive.

The Lettera 22 remained in production for 15 years (manufactured at Olivetti plants in Ivrea, Glasgow, Barcelona, Buenos Aires and Johannesburg). The sleek design was extremely influential and other companies produced similar designs.

Marcello Nizzoli (1887–1969) was a painter, designer and graphic artist. He worked as a graphic designer for Olivetti from the 1930s, creating a uniform corporate image. He became chief design consultant in 1936, a role he held for 22 years. Throughout this period Nizzoli's work for Olivetti led the industry in the adoption of advanced manufacturing processes, new materials and the highest standards in mechanical engineering.

His designs for typewriters and calculating machines are especially important, and draw heavily on organic and modernist forms. In 1954 he won the inaugural Compasso d'Oro Award, the pre-eminent Italian design award.

Nizzoli also worked as an architect for Olivetti, designing houses for employees, and office buildings for the company. He actively sought new challenges throughout his career, moving from painting to stage design, followed by a series of seminal designs for exhibitions, trade shows and retail shops.

61

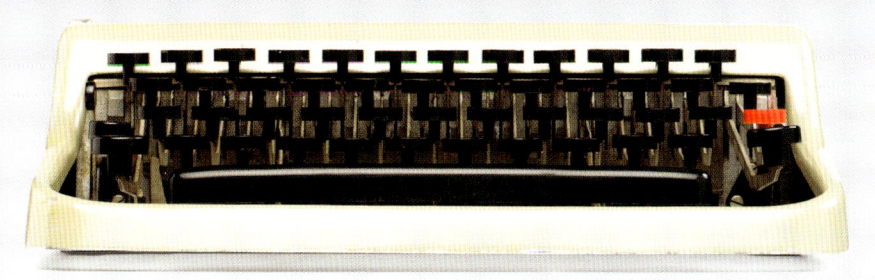

olivetti

MC24 DIVISUMMA CALCULATOR
Designed by Marcello Nizzoli and
Christmas Capellaro
Made by Olivetti
Italy, 1956
W: 240mm H: 260mm D: 420mm

The MC24 was the first calculator to employ a mode of use analogous to calculators as we know them today — with numbers and functions (add, subtract, multiply, divide) entered in sequence (3 + 4). This aspect of its operation alone made it simpler and more convenient than calculators employing non-sequential operation such as reverse Polish notation (3, 4, +).

In its mechanical engineering Olivetti used superior mounts, lubricants and metals machined within high tolerances to ensure quiet, reliable and long-life operation. An automatic electric calculating machine with integrated printing and register memory, the MC-24 remained in production for about 15 years. Over 1.5 million were produced in this period.

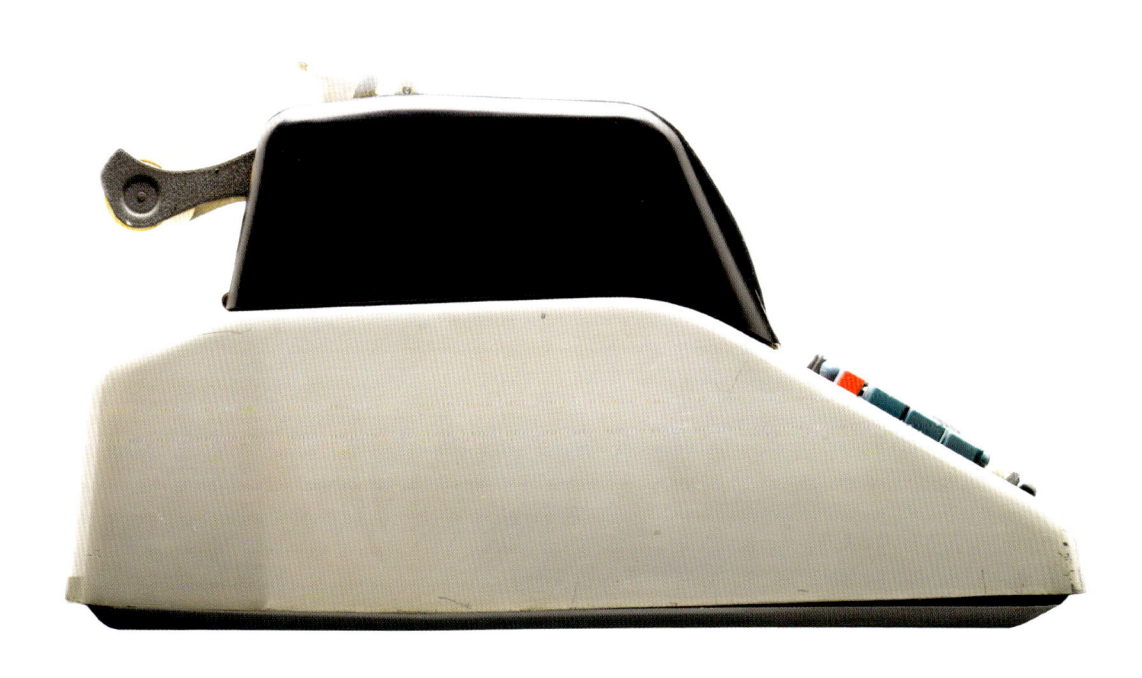

2+7 TELEPHONE
Designed by Marcello Nizzoli
Made by SAFNAT
Italy, 1958
L: 260mm W: 160mm H: 120mm

Marcello Nizzoli's design work was informed by a school of thought that sought to widen the role of industrial design within companies to encompass all aspects of product development from concept to production. Designers who adhered to this philosophy pursued a functionalist approach that abhorred ornament and saw the role of the designer to produce high quality goods for mass consumption that enriched peoples lives.

The Safnat telephone, designed by Nizzoli in 1958, demonstrates this approach to design. Its cellulose acetate housing, low-slung stature and anthropomorphic arrangement of dial and push buttons reflect Nizzoli's design attitude and methods; rejecting the accepted theories of machine design of the time ("form follows function"). Nizzoli's approach was to explore the interaction between the consumer and machine.

65

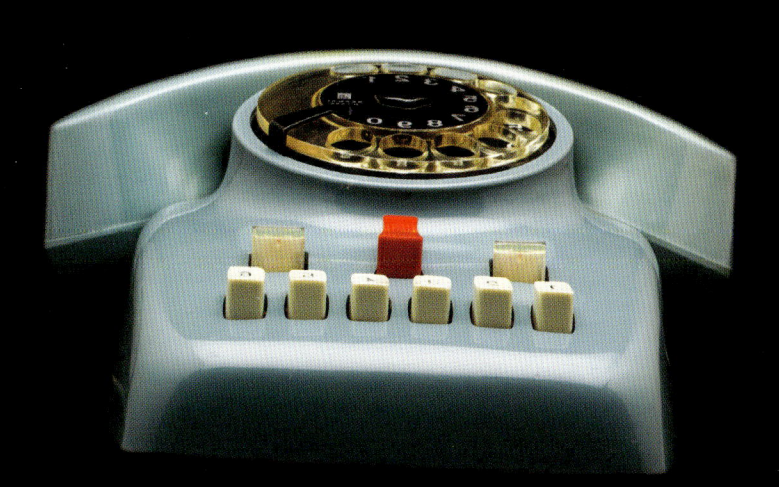

Artist Henry Moore explored the human form through increasing abstraction. Moore's early approach to his work, the manipulation of mass, is a method not dissimilar to Nizzoli's. Like Moore's abstracted and wrapped figures, seen here in *Reclining Figure 1976*, the telephone form is not abstracted beyond recognition.

c/a.   Moore

TRUB TELEPHONE
Made by Gfeller
Switzerland, 1972
W: 210mm H: 95mm D: 190mm

The casing of the Trub telephone is machined from a solid piece of rosewood. The use of a traditional material to realise a modern form for a technological device may have been a nod to the fine practice of Scandinavian furniture design. It may also have been a conscious decision by the manufacturer to produce a telephone that would sit well with modern furnished interiors incorporating similar materials. The Trub became a collectors' item, especially in Britain. When the company ceased manufacture and disappeared, reproductions began to be made. This example is from an early 1970s production run by Gfeller.

The metal call buttons are set to the right of the telephone face. This asymmetrical treatment may have been a practical consideration to accommodate internal components.

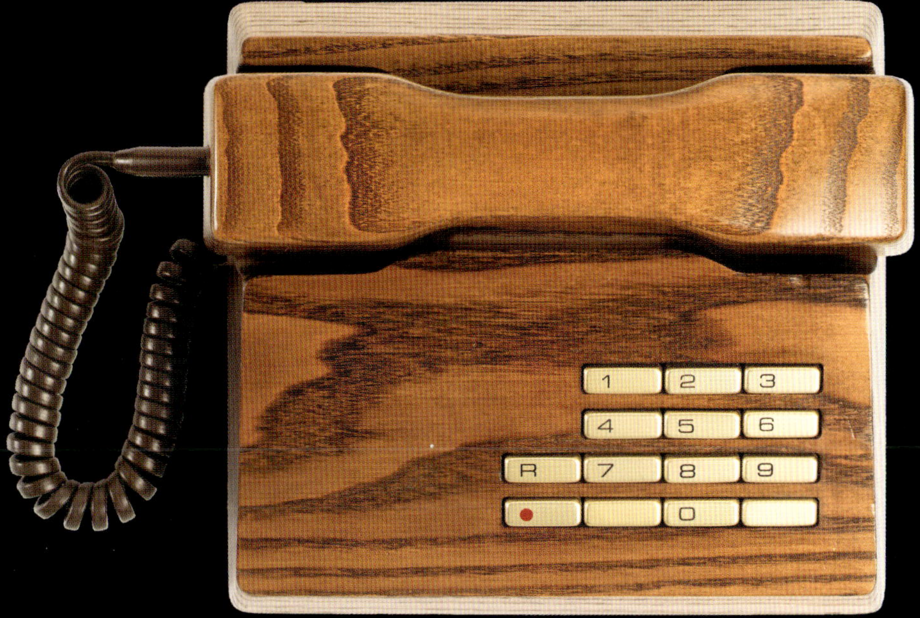
1 2 3
4 5 6
R 7 8 9
0

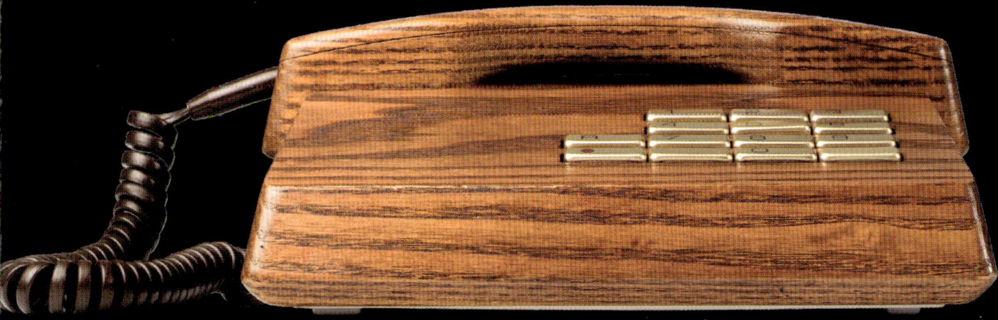

DANGER HIGH VOLTAGE IN POWER SUPPLY SECTION

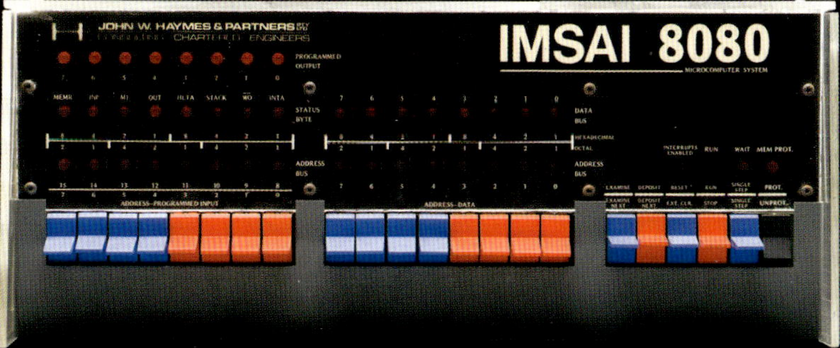
JOHN W. HAYMES & PARTNERS
CHARTERED ENGINEERS
IMSAI 8080
MICROCOMPUTER SYSTEM
PROGRAMMED OUTPUT
MEMR INP M1 OUT HLTA STACK WO INTA
STATUS BYTE
DATA BUS
HEXADECIMAL
OCTAL
ADDRESS BUS
INTERRUPTS ENABLED
RUN
WAIT
MEM PROT.
ADDRESS–PROGRAMMED INPUT
ADDRESS–DATA
EXAMINE
DEPOSIT
RESET
RUN
SINGLE STEP
PROT.
EXAMINE NEXT
DEPOSIT NEXT
EXT. CLR.
STOP
SINGLE STEP
UNPROT.

APPLE I PERSONAL COMPUTER
Designed by Steve Wozniak
Made by Apple Computer
USA, 1976
W: 320mm H: 450mm D: 105mm

Steve Wozniak (1950–), a computer hobbyist, was dabbling in computer design from high school. While working for Hewlett-Packard in the mid-1970s he built himself a computer using the new MOS technology 8-bit 6502 microprocessor and an old design for a video terminal for mainframe remote access.

In an environment dominated by computer kits with cumbersome input and output devices, Wozniak's computer represented a significant step towards a marketable personal computer. The design for what would become the Apple I employed an elegant economy of component architecture to perform the tasks of processing, generating video output and refreshing memory simultaneously, and it was easily connected to a keyboard. These differences made his computer simpler to use and cheaper to produce and sell than other kits available at the time.

Wozniak was showing off his design at a Homebrew computer club meeting in California and handing out schematics to people interested in building one when he ran into Steve Jobs (1955–2011), who suggested they sell it and within weeks he had an order for 100 kits from a local computer parts shop[4]. The production run for the Apple I was approximately 200. There are about 50 surviving examples in public and private collections worldwide. This is one of them.

The Blue Box was the first 'product' designed, produced and sold by Apple founders Steve Jobs and Steve Wozniak, who was then an employee of Hewlett-Packard. It allowed the user to make free telephone calls to anywhere in the world by generating the telephone company's 'secret' audio frequency tones. This early endeavour by the two Steves from 1972 heralded the beginnings of a partnership that was to later blossom in the development of Apple's early products[5].

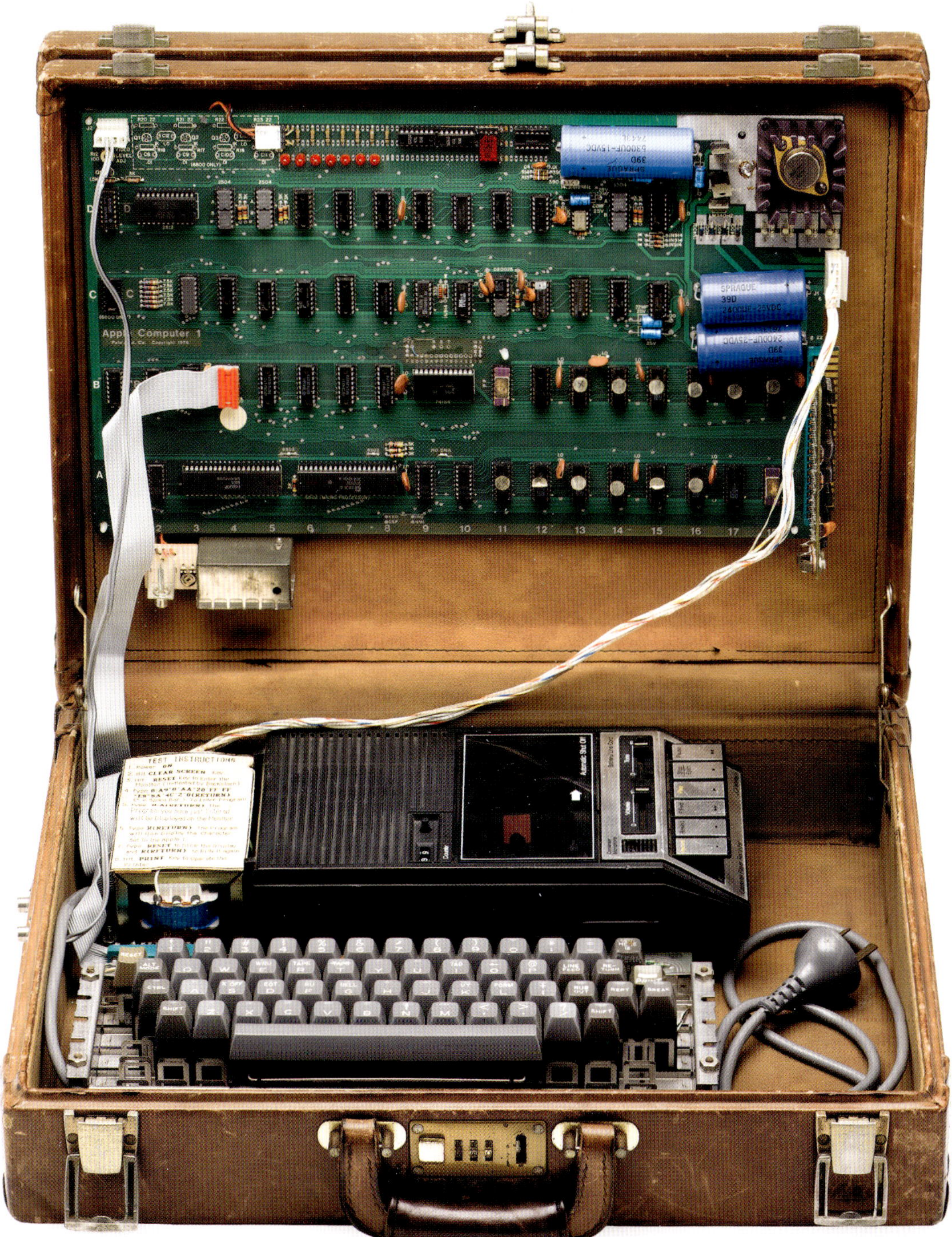
Apple Computer 1
SPRAGUE
39D
TEST INSTRUCTIONS

THE PROFESSIONALS

FROM USABILITY TO USER FRIENDLY

WHEN MAJOR COMPANIES DEVELOP INFORMATION TECHNOLOGY PRODUCTS FOR WIDESPREAD COMMERCIAL USE, THESE DEVICES ENTER THE SECOND PHASE OF 'ADOPTION'. DURING THIS PROFESSIONAL PHASE NEW DESIGN VALUES APPLY INCLUDING RELIABILITY, PERFORMANCE AND USABILITY. THIS SECTION FOCUSES LARGELY ON THE EFFORTS OF COMPANIES SUCH AS IBM, HEWLETT PACKARD, OLIVETTI, APPLE AND OTHERS TO DEVELOP SYSTEMS FOR OFFICE WORKERS AND PROFESSIONALS IN THE MID TO LATE 20TH CENTURY. IT ALSO HERALDS THE EMERGENCE OF 'DESIGN-LED' SOLUTIONS TO INFORMATION TECHNOLOGY DEVELOPMENT.

SELECTRIC 715 TYPEWRITER
Designed by Eliot Noyes
Made by International Business
Machines (IBM)
USA, 1961
W: 535mm H: 190mm D: 395mm

EXECUTARY DICTATION MACHINE
Made by IBM
USA, 1963–1968
W: 155mm H: 45mm D: 120mm

MAGNETIC BELT PACKAGING
Made by IBM
USA, 1963–1968
W: 210mm H: 16mm D: 120mm

New developments in office equipment through the second half of the 20th century brought about dramatic changes in office culture and the organisation of office labour. The Selectric typewriter went into production in 1961 following a 14-year development program at IBM that saw industrial design move from the office of Norman Bel Geddes to Eliot Noyes (1910–77), an American architect and industrial designer.

The Selectric typewriter and the Executary dictation machine were part of the vision of the IBM office products division (formerly its typewriter division) to develop 'start to end' technologies for the creation, distribution and printing of documents (word processing). IBM envisaged an office environment where word processing would be centralised and removed from other office activities.

The Selectric typewriter introduced the innovative 'golf ball' mechanism replacing type bars with a moving spherical printing element and eliminating the need for a moving carriage. The type mechanism is particularly sensitive to touch and responds with a weight and action that is apparently very satisfying.

In its heyday in the mid 1970s IBM Selectric typewriters accounted for around 75% of the US electric typewriter market. IBM's influence in this area began to decline following challenges from other manufacturers and new approaches to word processing. Xerox, Olivetti and later Apple all made inroads into the field.

IBM completely overhauled its products, packaging, stationary, advertising and corporate branding through the late 1950s to the early 1960s under the guidance of Noyes, regarded as a pioneer of integrating design and business strategy. The magnetic tape box displays IBM's visual identity from the 1960s. Designers involved in the project included Noyes alongside Marcel Breuer, Paul Rand and Charles Eames[1].

77

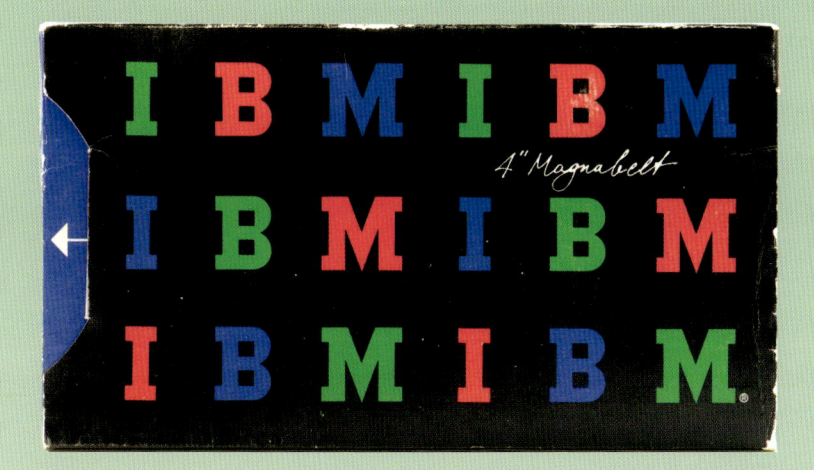

2250 DISPLAY UNIT
Made by IBM
USA, 1965
W: 1505 mm H: 1300mm D: 1685mm

The development of bit-mapped screens, where the computer retains a snapshot of the entire screen within memory, brought us one step closer to the computers we have today, which use bit-mapping technology to track all the objects on screen and our interaction with them.

The development of graphics and objects on screens in computer systems played a pivotal role in human-computer interaction. In the early years there were two schools of thought — one pursuing greater realism in graphic rendering, and the other using low-resolution images and objects as tools to increase useability of computers. The latter led to the development of the graphical user interface (GUI).

The IBM display unit used a bit-mapped screen and was designed to attach to an IBM 1130 computer system for computer-aided design purposes. Graphic and alphanumeric images were displayed as point-to-point vectors distributed over the 1024 x 1024 possible points the display was able to plot. Vectors could be modified through the use of an alphanumeric keyboard, the program-function keyboard or the light pen. The system could provide near instantaneous responses to commands to alter drawings and allowed for a conversational mode of interaction when developing solutions to computing tasks.

79

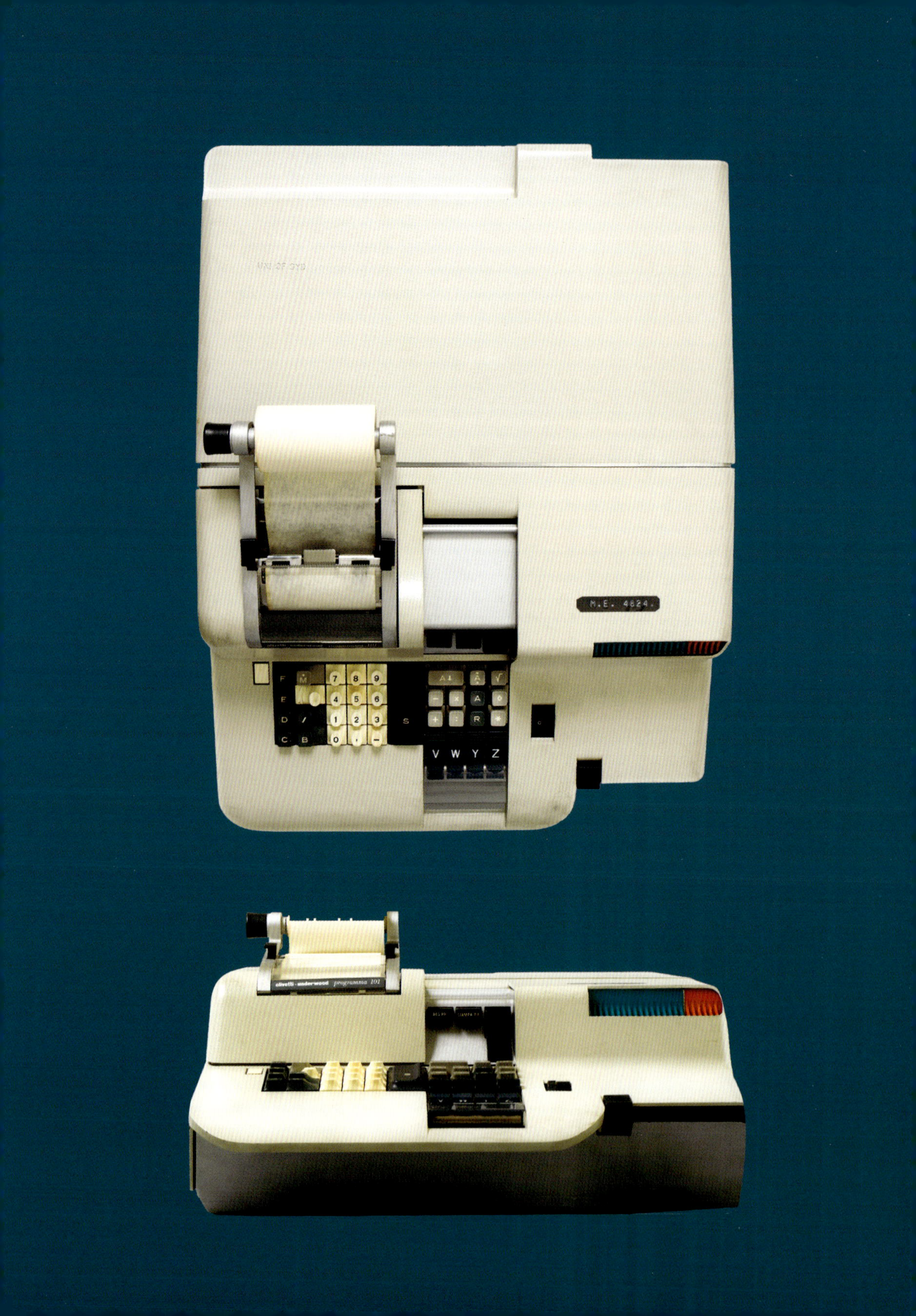
M.E. 4624.
olivetti-underwood programma 101
V W Y Z

PROGRAMMA 101 COMPUTER
Designed by Mario Bellini and Pier Giorgio Perotto
Made by Olivetti
Italy, 1965–1971
W: 465mm H: 275mm D: 610mm

Pier Giorgio Perotto (1930–2002) has long been regarded as the 'father of the PC' in Italy. He joined Olivetti in the late 1950s as part of its newly established electronics division. This division's task was to develop a computer, and the result was the first computer designed and manufactured in Italy, the Elea 9003 in 1959.

The Programma 101 grew out of a project that Perotto continued, without the endorsement of his managers, after Olivetti disposed of its electronics division in the early 1960s. Perotto's work drew upon his Elea experience and led to a product that helped Olivetti move beyond mechanical calculators.

It was released on the international market in 1965 as a low cost desktop computer. It was a successful product, selling over 44,000 units from 1965 through to the early 1970s. Ninety per cent of sales were to North America, where its market dominance was attributed to its simplicity, functionality, robust construction, appearance and low cost. The Programma 101's commercial life ended in the early 1970s with the introduction of compcting products, such as the Hewlett-Packard 9100.

The Programma 101 team at Olivetti with Perotto (front left) in the 1960s.

...information, c'est-à-dire impulsion qui élabore et produit l'information. L'information, c'est la logique et la puissance de calcul. Pour prévoir le volume des productions et des ventes, ou la taille moyenne des habitants de Vienne en 1999; pour déterminer la structure d'un viaduc ou l'aérodynamique d'une voiture de course. L'information, c'est l'impulsion magnétique qui, à partir d'une simple carte, instruit un ordinateur. L'information c'est l'impulsion électronique qui, à la vitesse de la lumière, voyage dans les circuits d'un ordinateur. Du micro-ordinateur qu'Olivetti a finalement installé sur votre propre bureau.

L'information passe par

Olivetti

Programma 101 - le premier micro-ordinateur à programmes enregistrés sur cartes magnétiques — P 203 - micro-ordinateur pour la gestion et l'administration des entreprises

"Information travels through Olivetti" advertisement designed by Igis Stucchi, 1969.

HP 9100A PROGRAMMABLE CALCULATOR (COMPUTER)
Made by Hewlett-Packard
USA, 1968
W: 410mm H: 210mm D: 490mm

The Hewlett-Packard 9100A is a small computer with a sophisticated instruction set on the keyboard ('software' built in as hardware). It was developed from prototype to pilot run of final instruments in just 10 months by the HP Industrial Design group, with cabinet styling by Roy Ozaki and Don Aupperle. Those involved in the design project described it as exothermic — which implies the process was not driven but simply evolved without great effort.

In the late 1960s, small commercial computers had no real precedents in product styling. Designers often turned to science fiction for their inspiration where these futuristic devices did exist. The other major influence on the appearance of high technology products was the US space program. Author Arthur C Clarke attributes the inspiration for the name of the computer in Stanley Kubrick's film *2001 A Space Odyssey* (1968), the HAL 9000, to the HP 9000 series of computers[2].

Hewlett-Packard was ordered to pay about $900,000 in royalties to Olivetti for their imitation of the Programma 101 magnetic card feature and architecture.

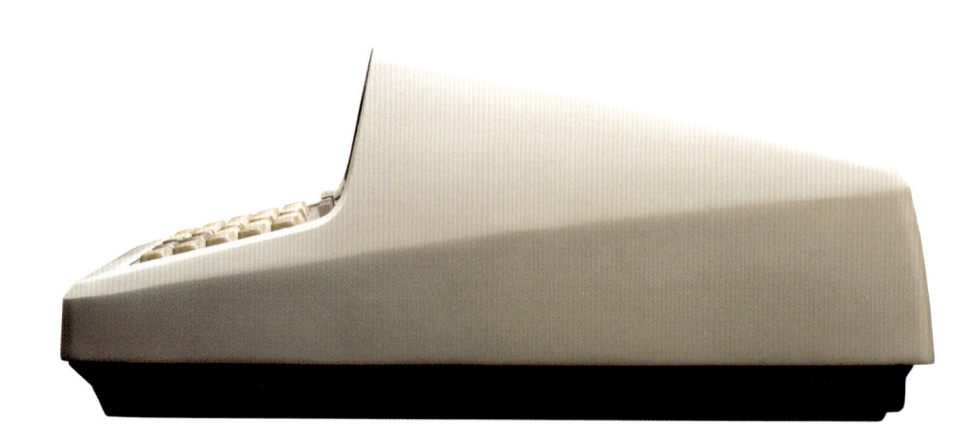

DEGREES
RADIANS
FLOATING
FIXED POINT
OFF
POWER ON
PROGRAM
RUN
DECIMAL DIGITS
CLEAR
PRINT
PAUSE
STOP
END

HP-65 CALCULATOR
Made by Hewlett-Packard
USA, 1974
W: 80mm H: 35mm D: 150mm

Six years after the launch of the HP 9100A computer, all its capabilities had been engineered into the HP-65 — the first programmable calculator designed to fit into a shirt pocket (hence the tapered form). It used magnetic strips to write, store and load programs and the multiple functions on each button gave the user almost immediate access to a multitude of operations.

Hewlett-Packard drew heavily on internal research and development for the HP-65. Mechanical and cognitive design studies resulted in a number of innovations: hinged keys pressing upon bent beryllium copper strips to provide a positive feel to their action; a card reader with a high level of stability ensuring reliable data writing and reading; 35 keys controlling in excess of 80 operations grouped into clusters according to their nature, with colour-coded nomenclature for multiple key-stroke operations; and key colour, size and value contrast designed to guide the user.

87

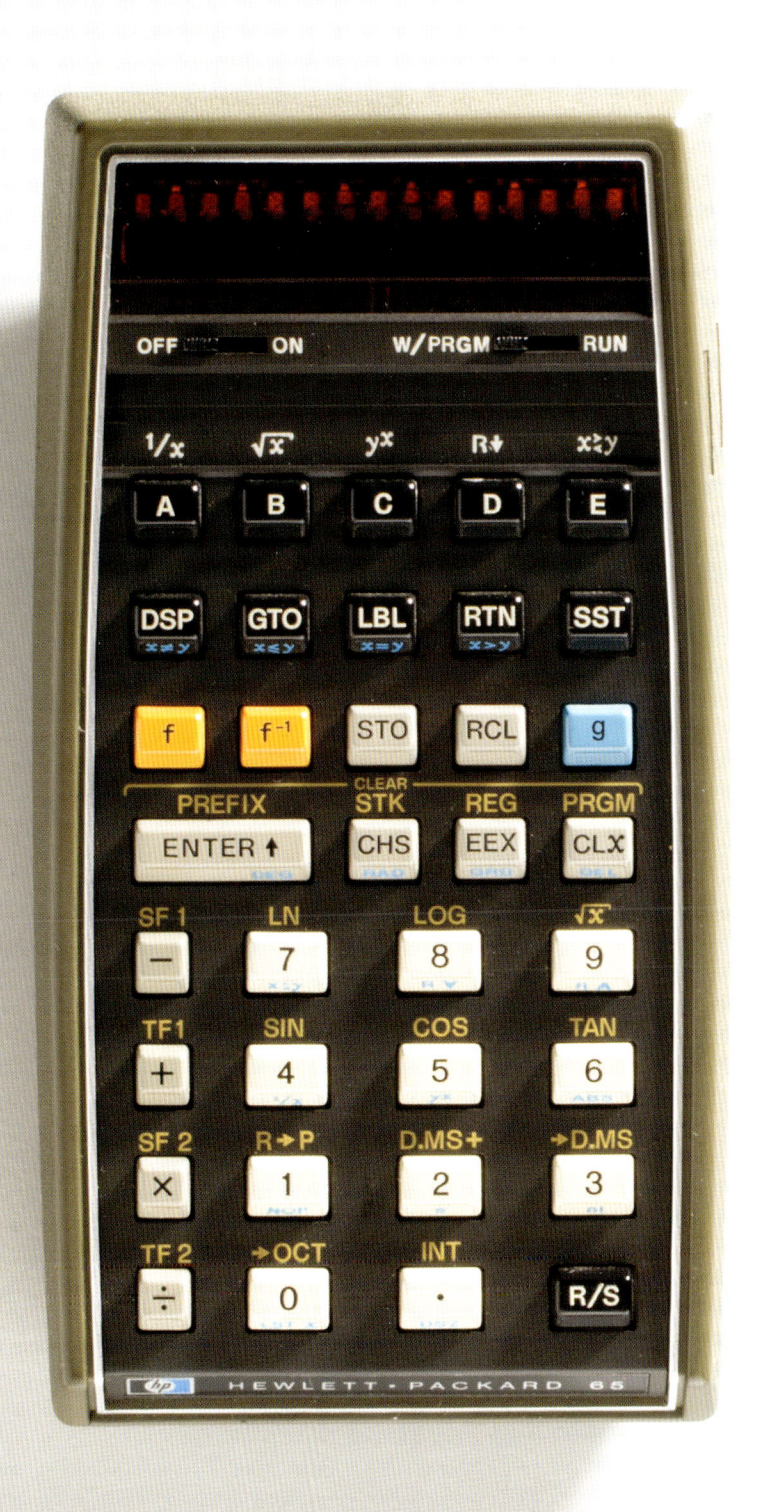

LETTERA 35 TYPEWRITER
Designed by Mario Bellini
Made by Olivetti
Italy, 1974
W: 345mm H: 110mm D: 350mm

Olivetti successfully fostered long term consultant relationships with some of Italy's finest industrial designers including Mario Bellini (1935–), who retained the position of chief design consultant from 1963 to 1991. Bellini's designs for Olivetti continued the company's tradition of exploring bold new forms for existing products. His design technique was to first build three dimensional models. He would then engage with and modify the prototype prior to any engineering drawings being executed. During this design process Bellini was able to refine the shape and visual impact, the product's narrative (an unfolding discovery of its abilities and use) and haptic or tactile properties.

With the accelerated uptake of rapid prototyping in the 1980s (where a CAD rendering could be machined almost instantly), this approach became popular with other manufacturers and designers.

The casing of the Lettera 35 is a study in carefully controlled form through plane, line and curve which echoes earlier treatments to Olivetti typewriter casings (such as the Ico), thus unifying its design within the larger body of Olivetti typewriters. Yet it clearly demonstrates Bellini's new found interpretation of existing forms.

The blunted Concorde nose mirrors the simple treatment of form at the typewriter's rear. The die cast aluminium casing joints are not flush leaving powerful visual lines along the side that emphasise the dropped nose. A slight fall in the type basket cover also exaggerates this form. A cheeky single red key presents a highlight while the eye-like platen roller knob offers a zoomorphic character to the profile.

LOGOS 55 DESKTOP CALCULATOR
Designed by Mario Bellini
Made by Olivetti
Italy, 1974
W: 430mm H: 125mm D: 255mm

Mario Bellini's design solution for this desk top calculator — a lectern-type wedge shape — could accommodate the mounting requirements of the printing mechanism and keep the keyboard input low and comfortable for the operator. The wedge shape is maintained by the recessed keyboard and the inset base, which creates the illusion of a floating form.

91

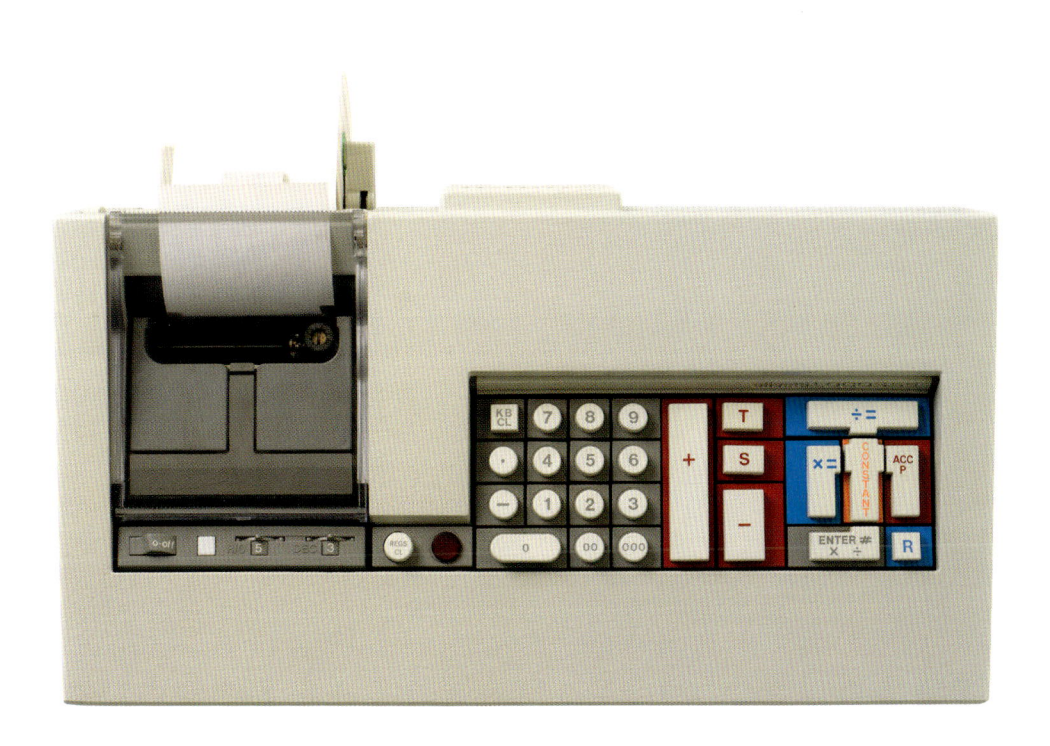

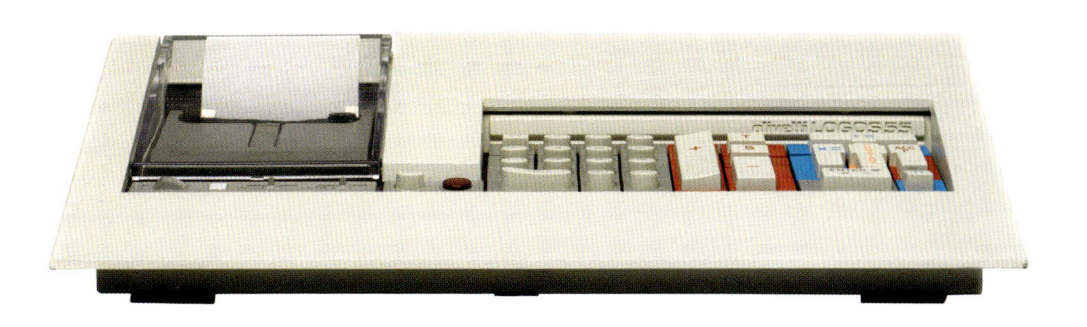

TES 501/55 WORD PROCESSOR
Designed by Ettore Sottsass
Made by Olivetti
Italy, 1976
W: 955mm H: 900mm D: 700mm

IBM's vision for office word processing was usurped by the introduction of machines like the Olivetti TES (Text Editing System) word processor. The user was able to generate documents, correct and print them. The large drives on the right hand side could be used to save or load documents. The machine could be used within a larger system of Olivetti devices for the control of information.

Ettore Sottsass (1917–2007) was an Italian architect and designer whose profound impact on design practice and thinking spanned half a century. Sottsass' design prowess moved effortlessly between designing complex information systems, such as Italy's first mainframe computer (Elea 9000) in the late 1950s, to modern ceramics. Sottsass thought deeply about design and its role within society and industry; he was profoundly influenced by travels to India and the United States, and he published and spoke widely on the topic of design.

93

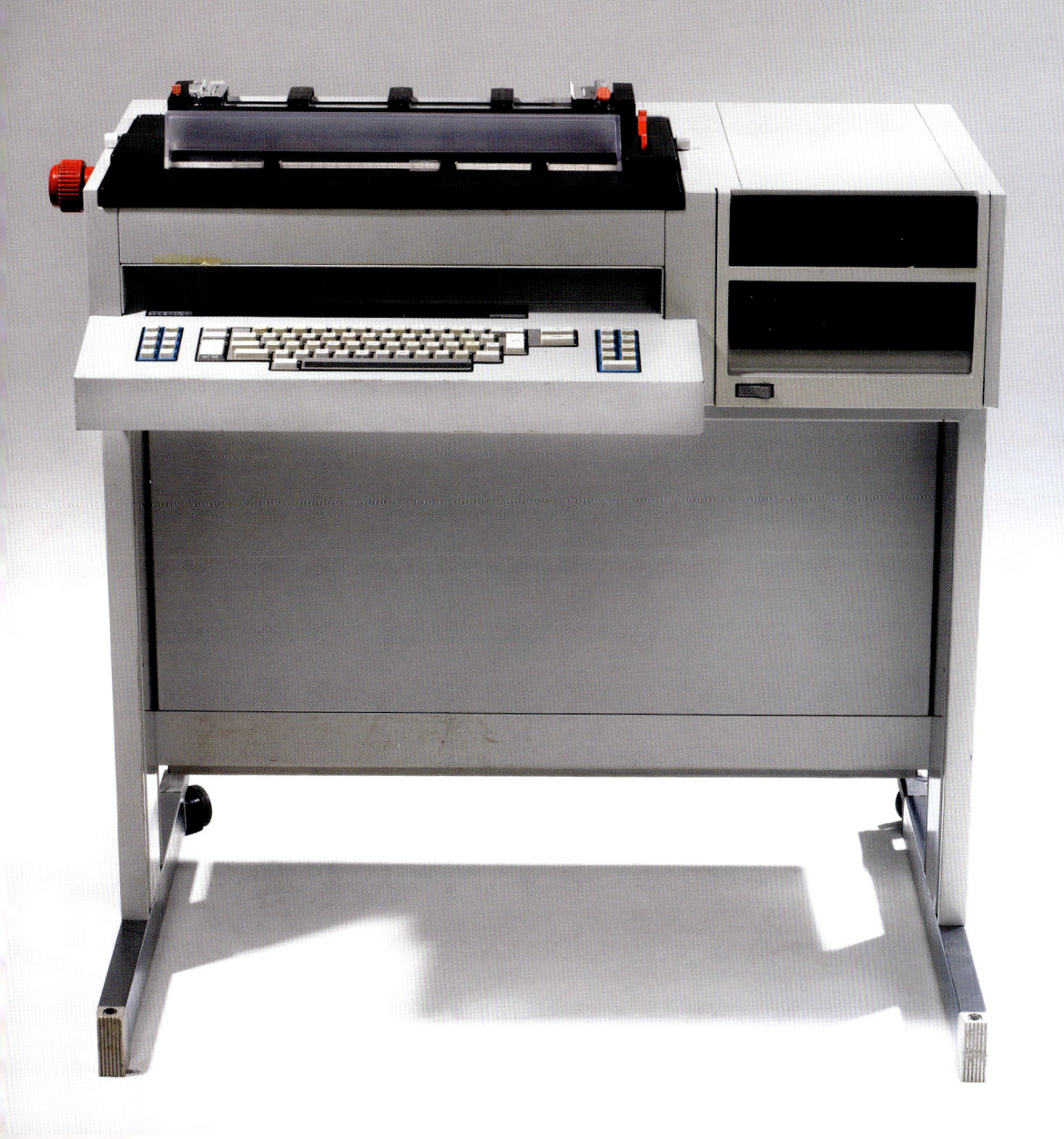

DASHER D2 COMPUTER TERMINAL
Made by Data General Corp
USA, 1977
W: 540mm H: 340mm D: 400mm

The D2 computer terminal is a cathode ray tube (CRT) designed for use with Data General mini-computers. Referred to as a dumb terminal or computer monitor, it is an interface device between people and computers in which communication is achieved by typed command lines which appear on a screen, with one line of text exchanged at a time.

The D2 is a descendant of the mechanical teletype (TTY), a device with a keyboard and printer that first appeared in the 1950s. The TTY was originally used in telecommunications where messages (telegrams) were digitised and sent to other remote TTYs. The mechanical TTY interface was eventually replaced by machines which used a screen to display text messages as they were exchanged.

The D2's design enables the rotation and pitching of the screen housing over a wide field through central axis points both vertical and horizontal. This type of design facilitates effortless adjustment.

CRTs offered many advantages over previous technologies. They did not use paper and ink and made less noise. They also permitted the editing of instructions on screen as the cursor could be repositioned to any part of the screen to erase and change information. Multiple fonts, colour and graphics were also available.

95

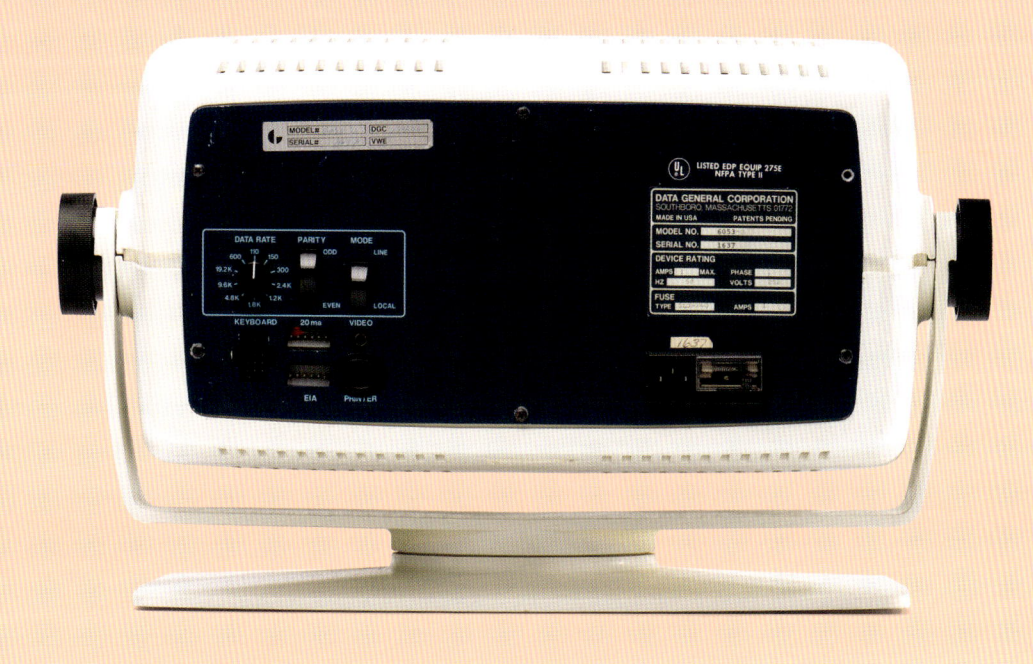

APPLE II COMPUTER
Designed by Steve Wozniak and Jerry Manock
Made by Apple Computer Inc
USA, 1977
W: 385mm H: 110mm D: 455mm

For his second personal computer Steve Wozniak produced an elegant and efficient circuit design with colour graphics (the first mass-market personal computer to do so). Although the Apple II launched without any compelling applications it was a design that, as Steve Jobs had hoped, would appeal to software writers and developers. The availability of Visicalc and the Apple II disk drive for the Apple II within months of its release helped propel sales through the late 1970s.

Steve Jobs hired Jerry Manock (1944–) to design the computer's housing. Manock had graduated from the Stanford Product Design Program and went to work for Hewlett-Packard (HP) where he was involved in the design of esoteric instruments for the microwave division. He left HP in 1972 and produced an electronic aid for the handicapped with Telesensory Systems before moving to Apple.

In 1977 cases for computers were rudimentary affairs cobbled together by owners from timber or made from blank metal cases supplied from electronics shop stock. Jobs was adamant that the Apple II case should be made of plastic because it would make the Apple II look more like a 'finished' mass-produced consumer product.

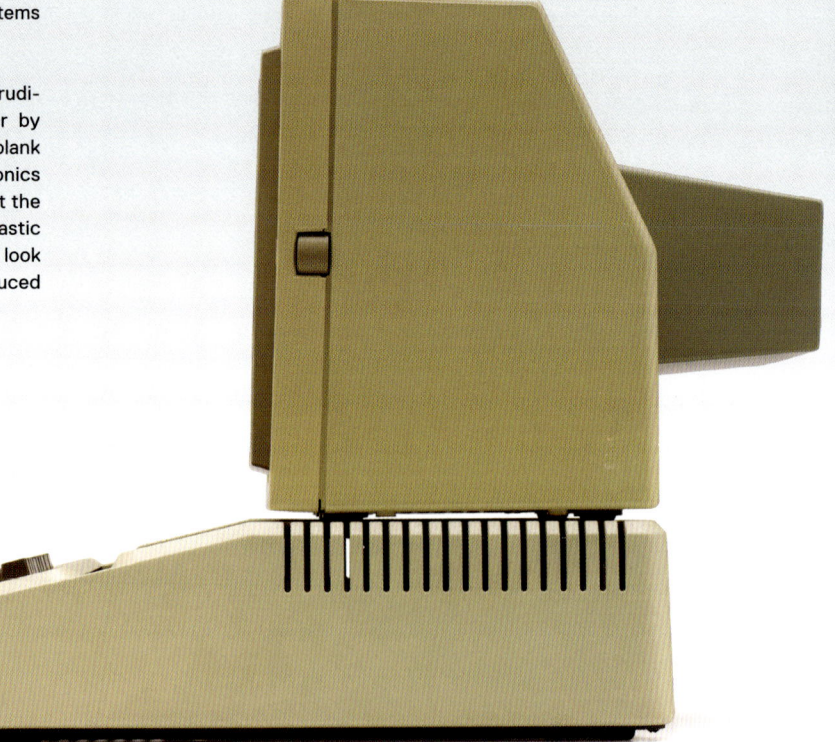

APPLE II MONITOR
Designed by Jerry Manock
Made by Apple Computer Inc
USA, 1982
W: 370mm H: 275mm D: 310mm

The Apple II provided a steady and growing stream of revenue from the late 1970s to the end of the 1980s. This revenue was particularly important to sustaining Apple's existence through protracted periods of research and development and product failures — in particular the Apple III and Lisa computers.

The monitor for the Apple II was released in 1982 nearly five years after the computer. Prior to its release most Apple II users fed the video output from the computer to whatever screen was available (television set, generic monitor). The Monitor II was a green phosphor monochrome tube mounted in a swivel bracket, enabling the user to adjust the screen angle. Despite its later release, the Monitor II remained in production until late 1993, thanks to the the longevity of the Apple II.

APPLE DISK II DISK DRIVE
Designed by Steve Wozniak
Apple Computer Inc
USA, 1978
W: 155mm H: 220mm D: 95mm

Disk drives were an expensive peripheral computer device (almost half the cost of the computer) so most people used a cassette for loading and writing data, which was a time consuming and often unreliable process. While at HP Wozniak had designed a floppy controller using only five chips. Other disk drive controllers at that time used about 50 chips. It went into production with about 30 assembled each day.

In early 1978 Visicalc, the first electronic spreadsheet program, became available for the Apple II. Developed by Bob Frankston and Dan Bricklin, Visicalc required 8K of memory to run, which outperformed Apple's main competitors (Commodore and Radio Shack). The combination of a lower cost floppy drive and the expandable memory of the Apple II, which was able to support 48K, helped sustain demand for the Apple II into the 1980s.

COMPUTER MOUSE (REPLICA)
Original designed by Doug Engelbart
Made by Bill English
USA, developed 1965, patent 1967
W: 110mm H: 70mm D: 85mm

Doug Engelbart (1925–2013) trained in electrical engineering and became one of the seminal figures of computer interface design. Inspired by the writings of American engineer and inventor Vannevar Bush, he set up the Augmentation Research Centre at Stanford Research Institute and set about developing new ways for people to directly interact with information.

By 1969 Engelbart and his team had looked at all the tools people used to interact with computers — keyboards, printers, screens, light pens and track balls — and had built some devices of their own, including the computer mouse. The mouse created a powerful interaction between people and computers. When the user moved the mouse in the real world, the pointer on the computer screen moved in the virtual world, mimicking the user's movements.

The original mouse was designed and built by Engelbart and Bill English at Stanford Research Institute and was named the 'X-Y Position Indicator for a Display System'.

ALTO COMPUTER
Designed by Charles P Thacker
Made by Xerox
USA, 1973

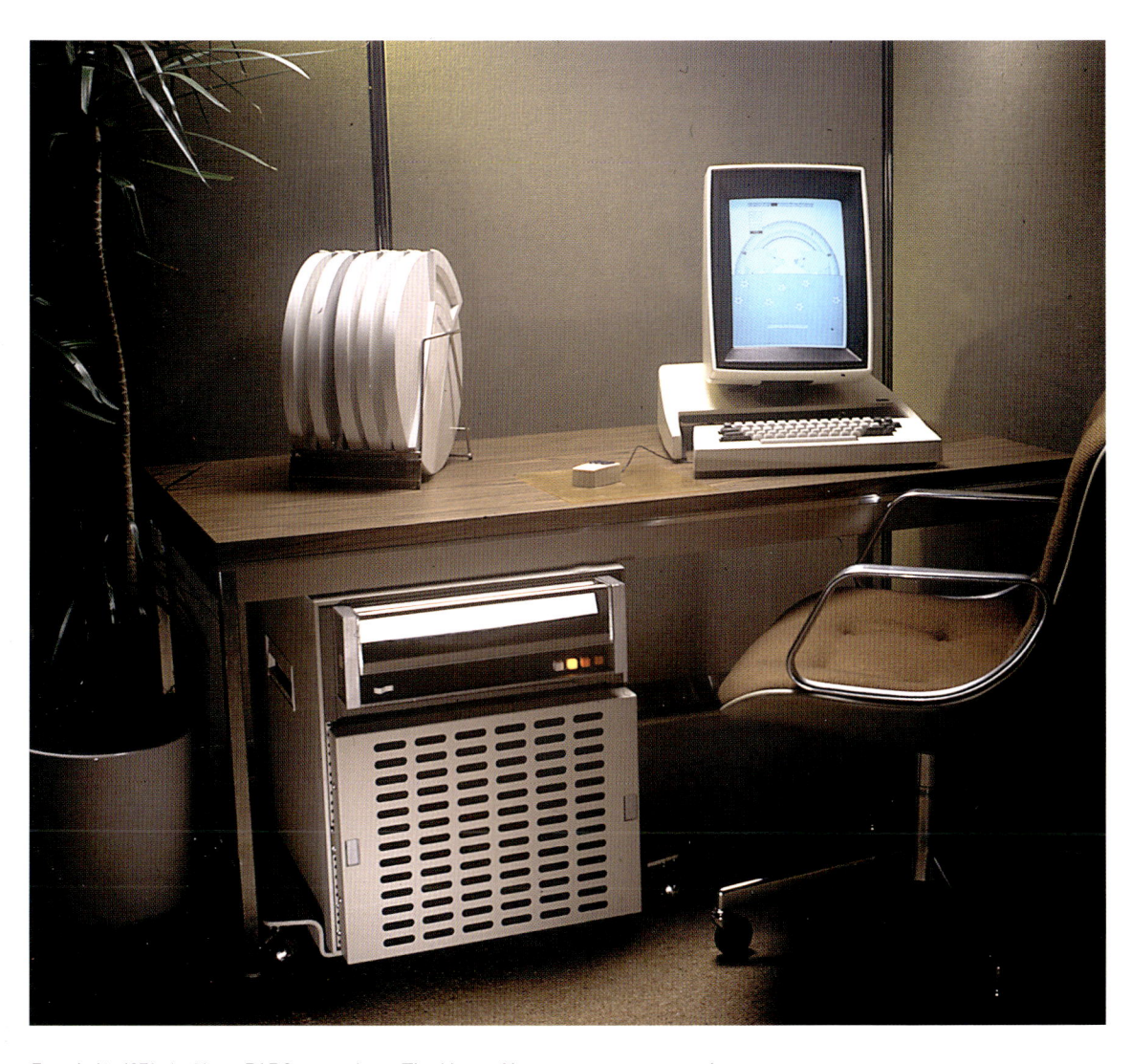

Founded in 1971, the Xerox PARC research facility in Palo Alto, California, developed and predicted key technologies that would be the cornerstone of the personal computer systems we now use — the graphical user interface, the mouse, being able to print exactly what appeared on the screen (WYSIWYG — what you see is what you get) and linking computers (Ethernet) so you could send and receive email, among other innovations. US computer scientist Alan Kay (1940–) developed the SmallTalk object-oriented programming environment at Xerox, an early GUI.

The Xerox Alto computer was used to demonstrate some of these developments to Steve Jobs and the Apple entourage in December 1979. Upon seeing the mouse being used with a graphical user interface (GUI) Jobs was transfixed — he understood that these were the tools non-computer users needed to interact with a computer.

Xerox tried to commercialise these technologies however the Xerox Star computer system was expensive. Despite this Xerox helped pave the way for the computer interface we use today.

MACINTOSH 128 PERSONAL COMPUTER
Designed by Jerry Manock, Terry Oyama, Steve Jobs, Ben Pang, Dave Roots, Lazlo Zeidek, Steve Balog, and Bill Bull
Made by Apple Computer Inc
USA, 1984
CPU and screen
W: 255mm H: 350mm D: 280mm
Keyboard
W: 345mm H: 80mm D: 160mm
Mouse
W: 65mm H: 35mm D: 100mm

The Macintosh was the first computer to successfully commercialise the graphical user interface (GUI) and the mouse. It was a huge shift in the development of human-computer interaction (HCI) — from purpose built machines to stored programs, interaction based on commands, screen forms and menus — and it escalated personal computer use.

According to Terry Oyama, one of the design team: "Steve (Jobs) thought about the Mac as an icon from day one. Even though Steve didn't draw any lines, his ideas and inspiration make the design what it is. To be honest, we didn't know what it meant for a computer to be 'friendly' until Steve told us." Apple launched the Mac with a television advertisement aired during the 1984 US Super Bowl[3].

The GUI became the standard method for delivering applications on Apple and PC platforms (especially after the release of Windows 3 in 1990, which saw the uptake of PCs by government agencies and business organisations). In 1986 when Apple launched Macs with four times more memory (the 512) — enough to run programs like Aldus PageMaker, Adobe Postscript, the Apple LaserWriter, Microsoft's Excel and Word for Macintosh — they became tools for the creative industries.

101

MACINTOSH ICONS
Designed by Susan Kare
Made by Apple Computer Inc
USA, 1984

Susan Kare (1954–), a fine arts graduate from New York University, moved to California when the call came from Apple for a graphic designer. Kare's trash can, folders, smiley Mac, command button symbol and other icons are reduced to just a few pixels (32 x 32) yet they remain recognisable.

Kare's influence on the look and feel of the graphical user interface extended to the appearance of the windows, drop down menus, dialogue boxes and fonts. All these elements were as crucial, influential and memorable in the success of the Macintosh system as any of the engineering and product design feats accomplished by the Macintosh design team.

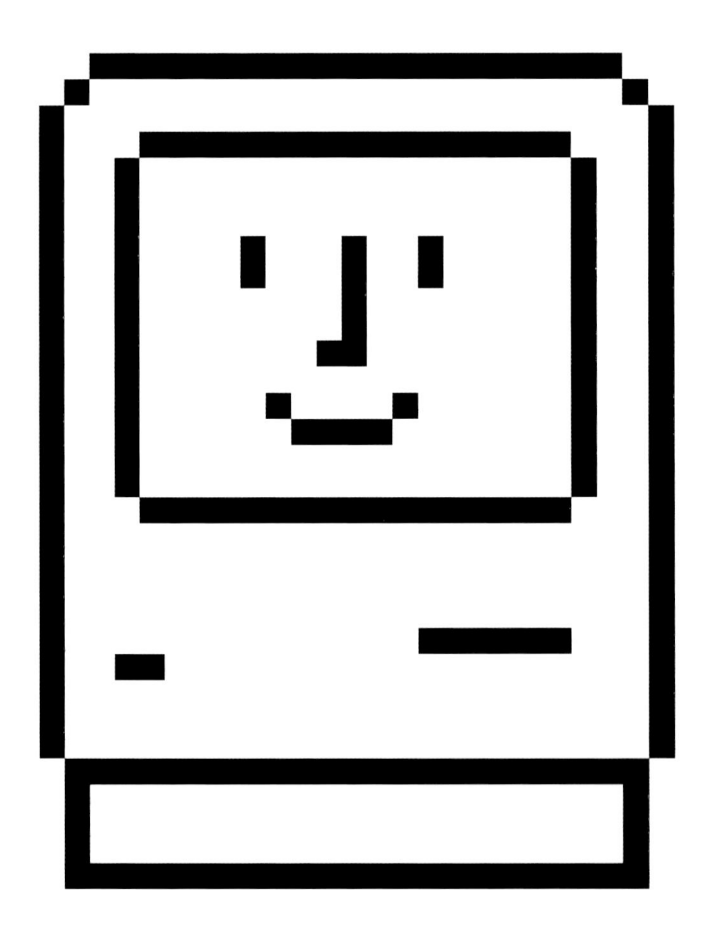

103

APPLE IIC COMPUTER
Designed by Hartmut Esslinger
Made by Apple Computer Inc
USA, 1984
W: 290mm H: 320mm D: 540mm
assembled

In the early 1980s Steve Jobs set up a design competition to find the best candidate for Chief Industrial Design consultant at Apple. Jobs understood that great design could play a pivotal role in transforming Apple into a global brand with a unified product and corporate identity. He chose the frog design group headed by German-born Hartmut Esslinger (1944–), who relocated from Germany to North America to undertake the work. The Apple IIc was the first product to display all the attributes of the 'Snow White' design language developed by Esslinger for Apple products.

The Snow White design scheme uses horizontal and vertical stripes on enclosures to give an illusion of reduced volume to the parts; a three dimensional Apple logo inlaid into product cases; an off-white colour scheme; and the product name printed onto the surface.

Introduced alongside the new Macintosh in January 1984, it assured existing customers that the Apple II line of products would not disappear in the Macintosh revolution. The Apple IIc was an extremely popular machine, selling over 400,000 units by the end of 1984. Apple II products continued to bring in the greater portion of revenue until the early 1990s when the Macintosh overtook its predecessor.

105

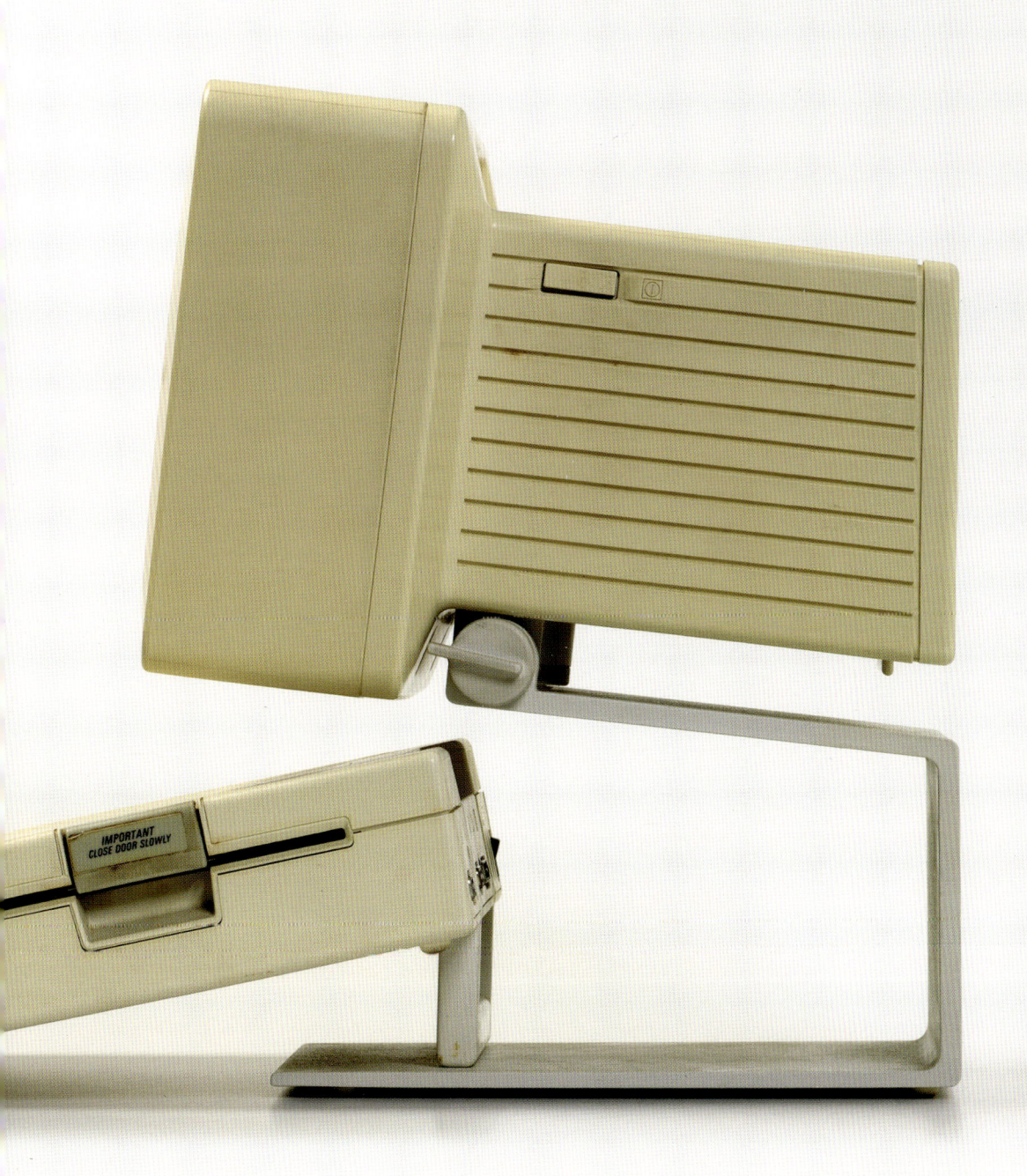

on/off
select
print quality
line feed
form feed
paper
ImageWriter II

ImageWriter II

IMAGEWRITER II
DOT MATRIX PRINTER
Designed by Bill MacKenzie and
Mark Pruitt (Apple), Stephen Peart
and Hartmut Esslinger (frog design)
Made by Apple Computer Inc
USA, 1985
W: 460mm H: 170mm D: 325mm

The ImageWriter II demonstrates the implementation of the Snow White design language, developed by Hartmut Esslinger's frog design, on an existing Apple product. Snow White established a set of parameters that all Apple products were to follow and although the details may seem appearance-driven they also "served a structural or functional purpose".[4]

The profile of the ImageWriter is a direct homage to Mario Bellini's Olivetti designs from the 1970s, reminiscent of the Logos series of desktop printing calculators. Designer Stephen Peart (frog design), recalled: "I asked myself, 'What if I was sitting in Olivetti's studio and Mario Bellini asked me to design a dot-matrix printer? What would I do?'"

Stephen Peart describes the final design review presentation: "[Jobs] looked at it for about five seconds and said, 'Has Bill MacKenzie (Apple Industrial Design) seen this?' Peart nodded, at which point Jobs said, 'Looks great. Build it.'"[5]

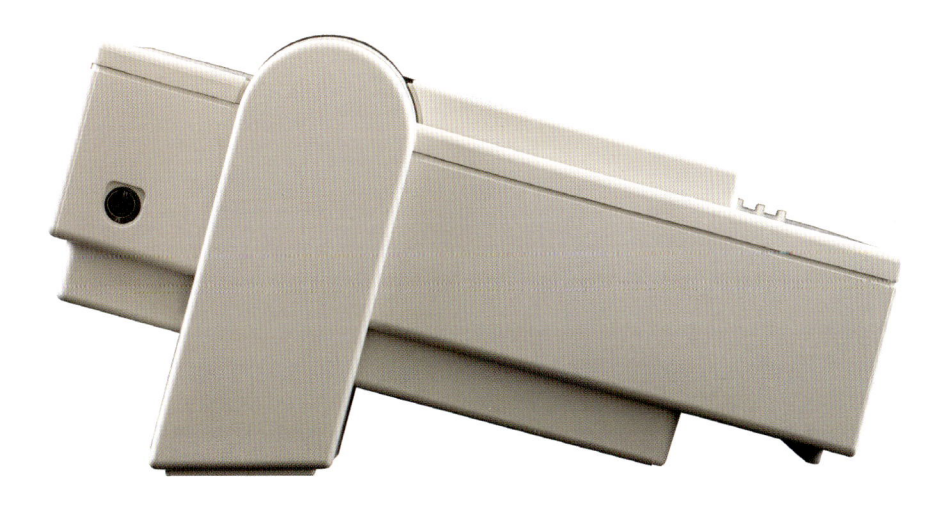

NEXT COMPUTER CENTRAL
PROCESSING UNIT
Designed by Hartmut Esslinger
Made by NeXT Inc
USA, 1988
W: 305mm H: 305mm D: 305mm

After he was ousted from Apple Computer in 1985, Steve Jobs' pet project (alongside Pixar) was the NeXT computer. Jobs wanted to build a cheap supercomputer for academics and scientists who were frustrated by time-sharing on mainframe systems they were then using. This was Jobs' attempt to set a new standard in computing as the pace of innovation in the industry slowed.

The NeXT operating system and development environment were superior, using nascent object technology which let users assemble their own applications simply and easily. The NeXT system also employed Motorola processors that were faster than any Mac or PC and used optical disk storage. All this was packaged in a die-cast magnesium cube designed by Hartmut Esslinger.

The NeXT computer was the device on which Tim Berners-Lee developed a system for linking academics across the internet using hypertext, which became known as the World Wide Web. "The NeXT interface was beautiful, smooth and consistent," said Berners-Lee, and "it also had software to create a hypertext program"[6].

In 1989, when Steve Jobs was questioned over delays to the launch of NeXT he replied: "Late? This computer is five years ahead of its time."[7]

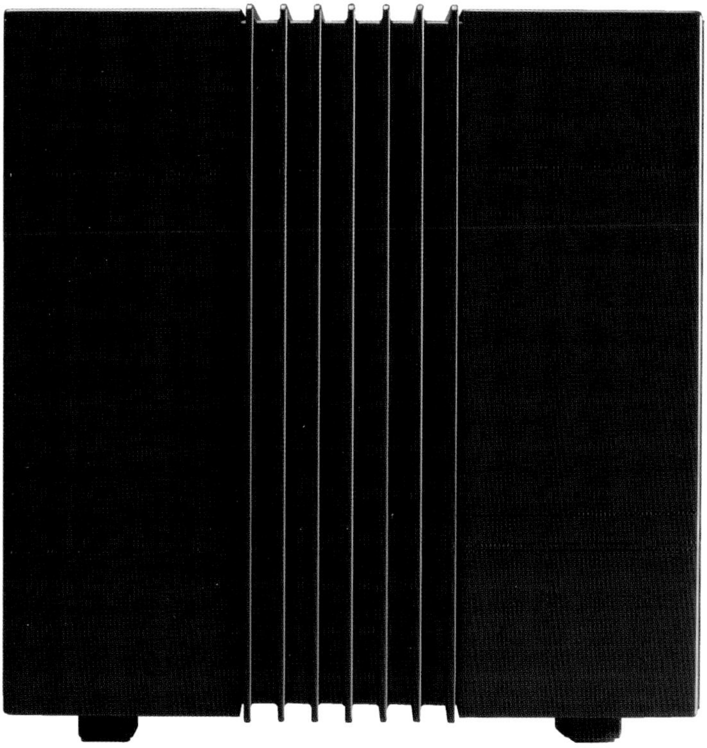

THE CONSUMERS

FORM FOLLOWS EMOTION

THE DESIGN PHILOSOPHY CHAMPIONED BY MARIO BELLINI AND OTHERS SOUGHT TO SUPPRESS THE TECHNICAL DIMENSION OF INFORMATION TECHNOLOGY PRODUCTS. DEVICES BECAME MORE PLAYFUL, PERSONAL, AND OFTEN MORE MOBILE. WHEN THE EXPERIENCE OF USING A DEVICE IS HUMANISED IN THIS WAY, IT BECOMES INTUITIVE TO THE USER. DURING THIS THIRD PHASE OF ADOPTION CONSUMER UPTAKE ACCELERATES. THIS SECTION SHOWCASES SOME OF THE GREAT CONSUMER PRODUCTS OF THE SECOND HALF OF THE 20TH AND EARLY 21ST CENTURIES.

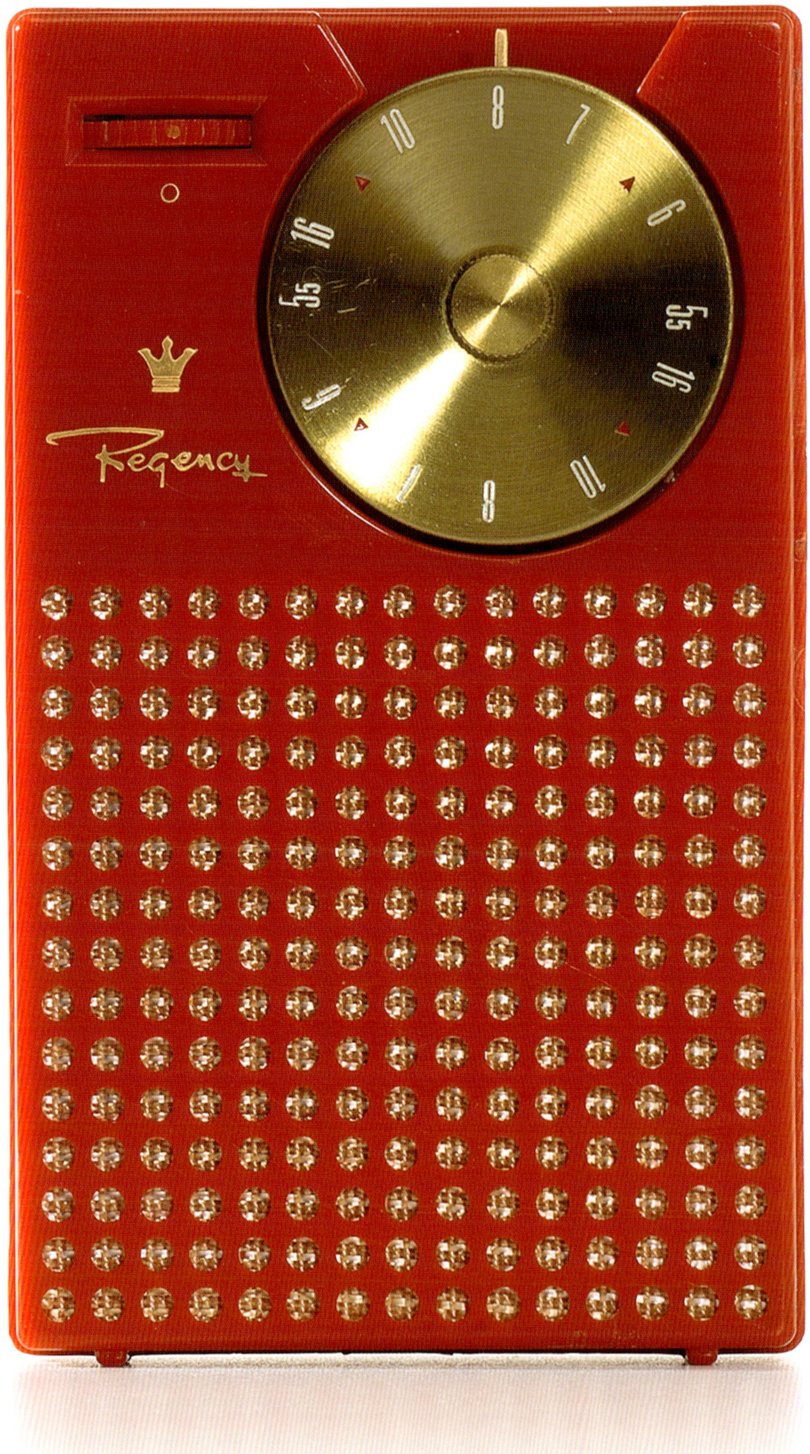
Regency

TRANSISTOR RADIO
Designed by Painter, Teague & Petertil
Made by Regency Division IDEA Inc
USA, 1954–1958
W: 76mm H: 127mm D: 34mm

In July 1954 Texas Instruments and Industrial Development Engineering Associates (IDEA) embarked on a project to produce a pocket-sized radio for the Christmas market. The result was the Regency TR-1, the world's first pocket radio. Over 100,000 were sold during its first year of manufacture in a range of colours[1].

A radio of this size was made possible by the development in 1948 of a solid state amplifier — the transistor — by William Shockley, Walter Brattain and John Bardeen. Up until this time the vacuum tubes used in the electronic circuits of radios required more space and power to run them.

The Regency radio's simple shape, perforated grille and tuning wheel presented a set of solutions that were imitated by almost all pocket radios that followed.

This 1950s advertisement for the Regency emphasises its then novel features: size and portability.

RT20 RADIO
Designed by Dieter Rams
Made by Braun
Germany, 1961
W: 500mm H: 260mm D: 180mm

The design of the RT20 radio is based on the design idiom Dieter Rams established with Hans Gugelot to produce the SK4 radiogram in 1956. Made from beech with coated sheet steel, the RT20 was the last tabletop radio produced for Braun.

The RT20 is a composition of circles and rectangles, with lines reconciled within circles (the speaker grill) and circles reconciled within lines (the buttons and knobs). The form is consistently evolved from only these elements. This reduction produces a unifying balance to the surface and coherence to the controls.

German industrial designer Dieter Rams (1932–) joined Braun in 1955 as an architect and an interior designer. In 1961 he was appointed Chief Design Officer, a position he held until 1995. Rams' designs for Braun are a product of the analytical rationalist method inherited from the Ulm School of Design. They demonstrate the orderly treatment of form and materials. By removing elements vying for the user's attention, the devices present clarity[2].

PHONOSUPER RADIOGRAM
Designed by Hans Gugelot and Dieter Rams
Made by Braun AG
Germany, 1963
W: 290mm H: 245mm D: 585mm

Revolutionary in its appearance, the SK55 Phonosuper epitomised Braun's efforts to transform and differentiate the image of the company and its products from manufacturers of dowdy brown timber-cased radios with cloth grilles.

The Phonosuper was a direct descendent of the SK4 radiogram, released seven years earlier and also designed by Gugelot and Rams. With its clear acrylic lid and white-lacquered sheet metal body, the design defied existing notions of what a gramophone should look like. Nicknamed 'Snow White's coffin' by its detractors, it was embraced by consumers and firmly established Braun's reputation in contemporary design.

A German designer of Dutch descent, Hans Gugelot (1920–65) was an influential lecturer at the Ulm School of Design from 1954 until his death in 1965. He is best known for his modular office furniture designs and his appliances for Braun.

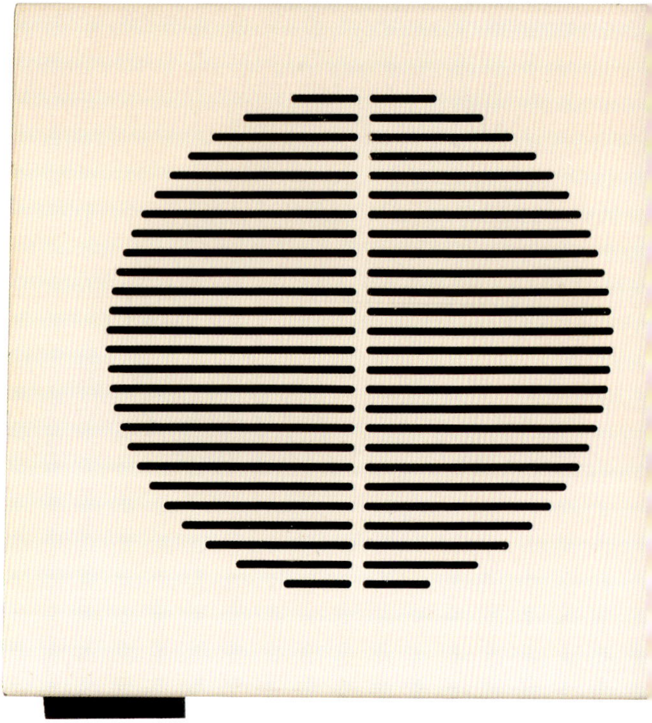

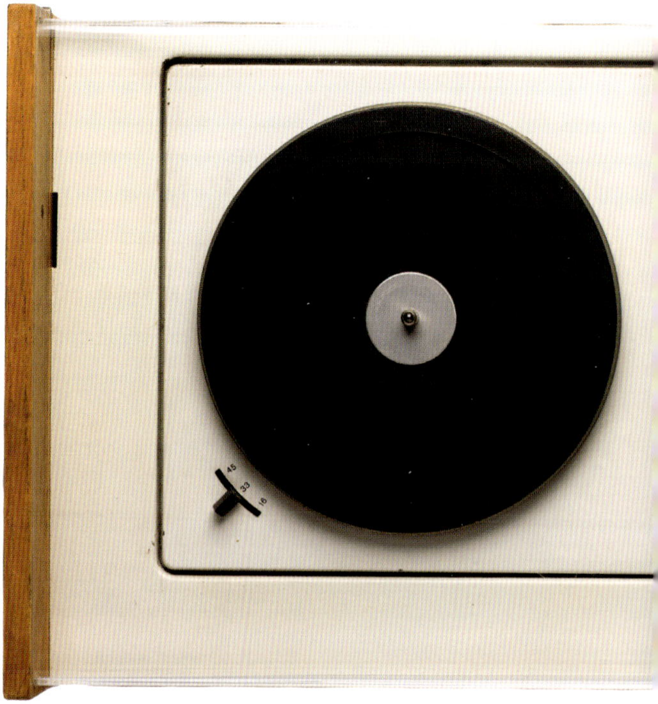
45
33
16

BRAUN
höhen
tiefen
volumen
ein aus
phono
lang
mittel
ukw
sender

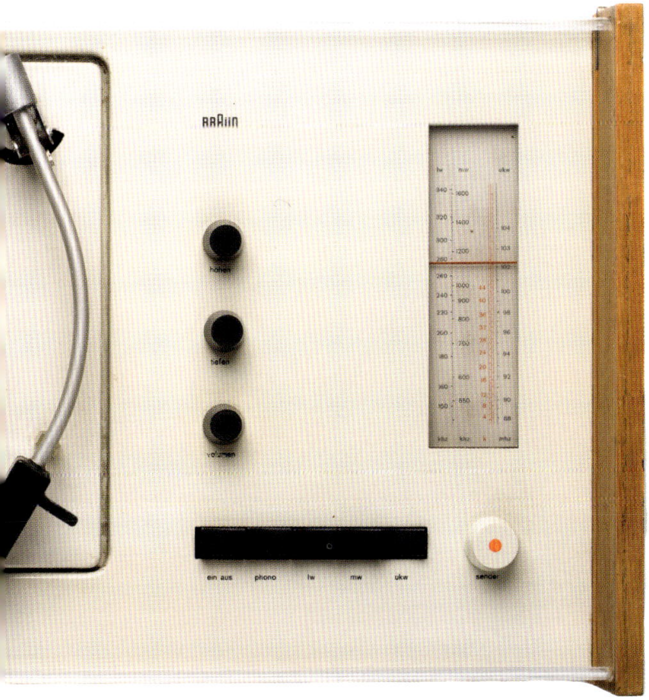
BRAUN
höhen
tiefen
volumen
ein aus
phono
lw
mw
ukw
sender

T1000 WELTEMPFAENGER (WORLD RECEIVER) RADIO
Designed by Dieter Rams
Made by Braun GmbH
Germany, 1963
W: 360mm H: 300mm D: 120mm

The T1000 embodies Rams' belief that well designed products (that have resolved a form for simplicity, intelligibility, utility and longevity) can promote democracy. In the early 1960s, as Germany was emerging from the chaos of World War II, the T1000 radio enabled access to the world with its extraordinary bandwidth and mobility, while its physical form presented order, harmony and economy (three design ideals favoured by Braun from this period). The T1000 stands out for its engineering — the radio was capable of scanning all available broadcasting frequencies — and its restrained physical appearance — when closed the case of anodised and lacquered aluminium presents a unified exterior.

The idea that good design promotes democracy was advocated throughout the Cold War years (1945–70). However East and West both engaged in an ideological and aesthetic battle to "demonstrate a superior vision of modernity" through design[3]. Roman Cieslewicz's 1968 *Superman* poster illustrates the argument.

119

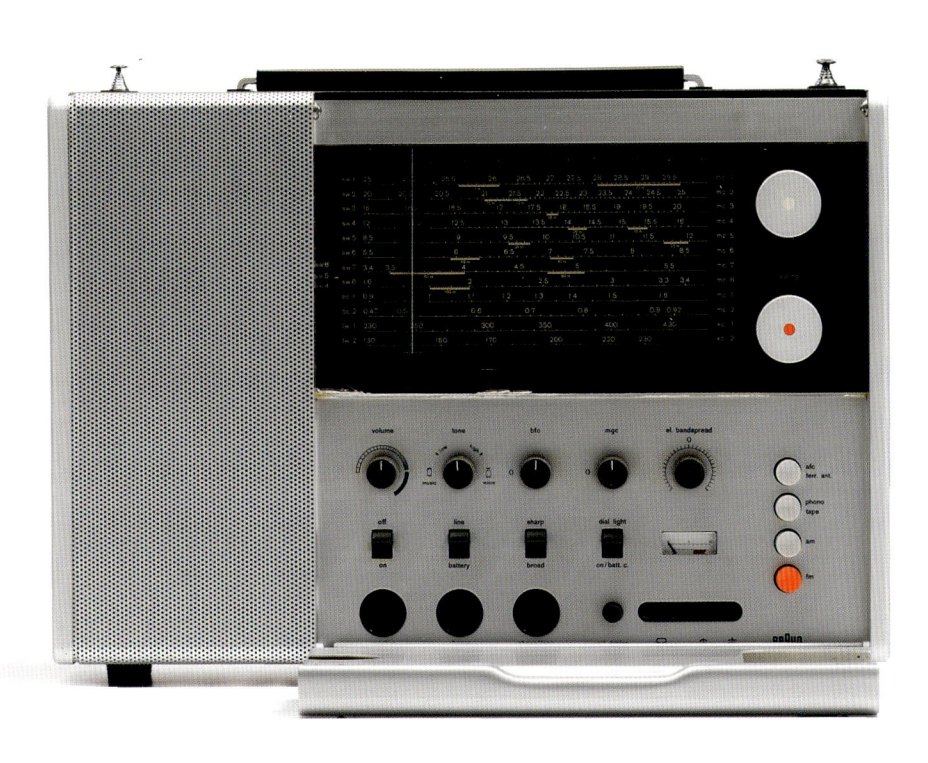

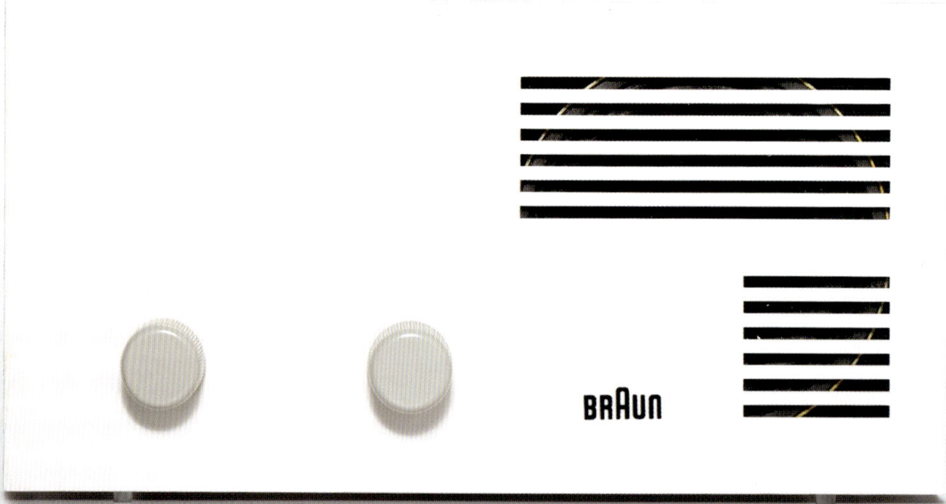
BRAUN

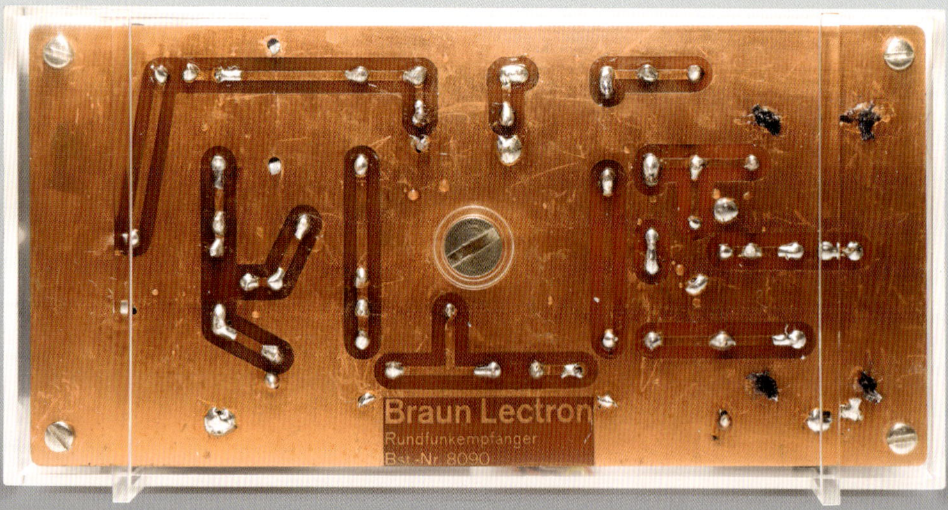
Braun Lectron
Rundfunkempfänger
Bst.-Nr. 8090

LECTRON RADIO RECEIVER
Designed by Dieter Rams and Jurgen Greubel
Made by Braun AG
Germany, 1967
W: 162mm H: 81mm D: 46mm

This kit product was designed for the enthusiast who understood electronic circuitry and knew how to solder. Nonetheless the designers considered the performance, function and appearance of the assembled product as important as any other Braun appliance. The kit came with advanced components, including a mercury switch, which activated the radio when shifted from lying flat to standing upright and eliminated the need for a physical switch.

In the late 1950s through the 1960s Braun built its design image on its range of audio appliances. Braun entered the hi-fi field after its competitors in the USA and UK, with a clear strategy to capture a share of the market. The company's superior design, executed through the economic application of new materials, ensured its initial success. Braun's later system design, demonstrated in its component approach to audio products, maintained the market penetration.

RR 126 STEREO RADIOGRAM
Designed by Achille and Pier Giacomo Castiglioni
Made by Brionvega
Italy, 1966
W: 1240mm H: 750mm D: 365mm

The Brionvega RR126 was nicknamed the Musical Pet because of its zoomorphic features — the symmetrical arrangement of the dials and controls, the pedestal legs with castors and speakers hung on the sides like ears.

The Castiglioni brothers, Achille and Pier, believed the redesign of an existing product required investigation of the available technologies and materials followed by the identification of a Principal Design Component (PDC). The PDC could be anything from new technology to changing behaviour. This led them to radically rethink all the products that they were commissioned to design, often restructuring an object's function, form and production process[4].

Brionvega was one of many Italian manufacturers of domestic consumer goods that encouraged flamboyance in product design, without deviating too far from function. The company worked with outstanding Italian industrial designers, among them Marco Zanuso, Richard Sapper, Mario Bellini and Ettore Sottsass.

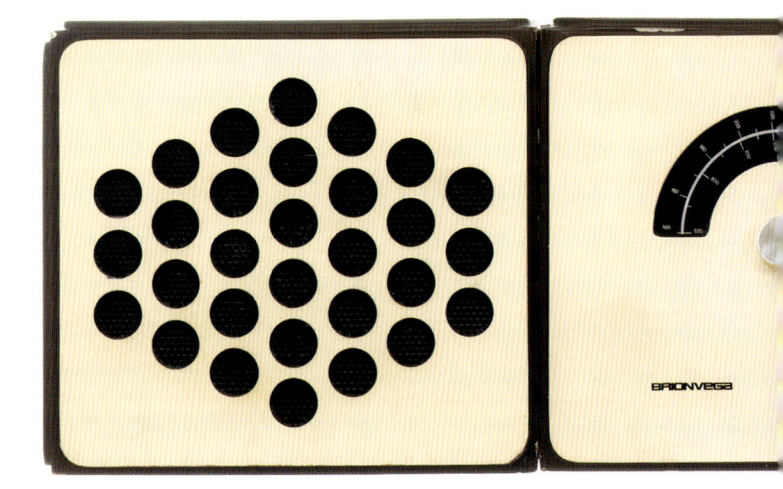

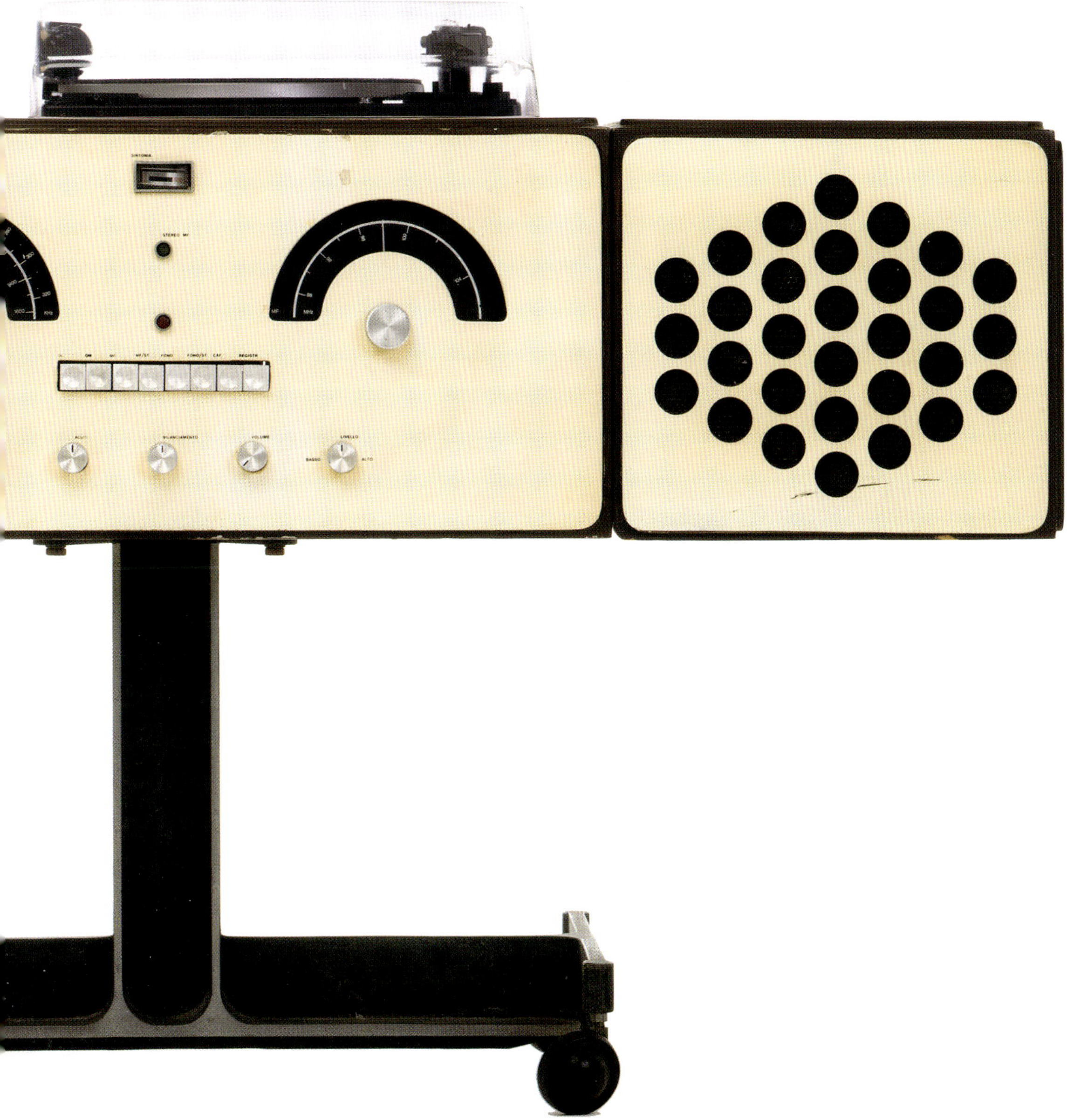
SINTONIA
STEREO MF
MF
MHz
KHz
OM
MF/ST
FONO
FONO/ST
CAF
REGISTR
ACUTI
BILANCIAMENTO
VOLUME
LIVELLO
BASSO
ALTO

VALENTINE TYPEWRITER
Designed by Ettore Sottsass and Perry King
Made by Olivetti
Italy, 1969
W: 340mm H: 100mm D: 340mm

Designer Ettore Sottsass took a simple machine, the portable typewriter, and encased it in bright red plastic to create the Valentine. Previous designers for Olivetti had produced revolutionary forms that helped demolish popular prejudices about office equipment, in turn promoting these machines for wider use and consumption. Sottsass took the process one step further and transformed a useful object into a lifestyle accessory.

In the 1960s Sottsass became disillusioned with the role of the designer in supporting consumer products. He was involved in the neo-avant guard, a radical period in Italian design thinking. One group to emerge from this was Superarchitettura, which sought to combine the inventiveness of pop art with the dynamics of mass production. From this Sottsass extracted an 'anti-banalising' treatment for the typewriter.

In this 1970 poster for the Valentine, US graphic designer Milton Glaser has inserted the typewriter into Piero di Cosimo's Renaissance painting *The Death of Procris*, seemingly elevating the machine to a work of art.

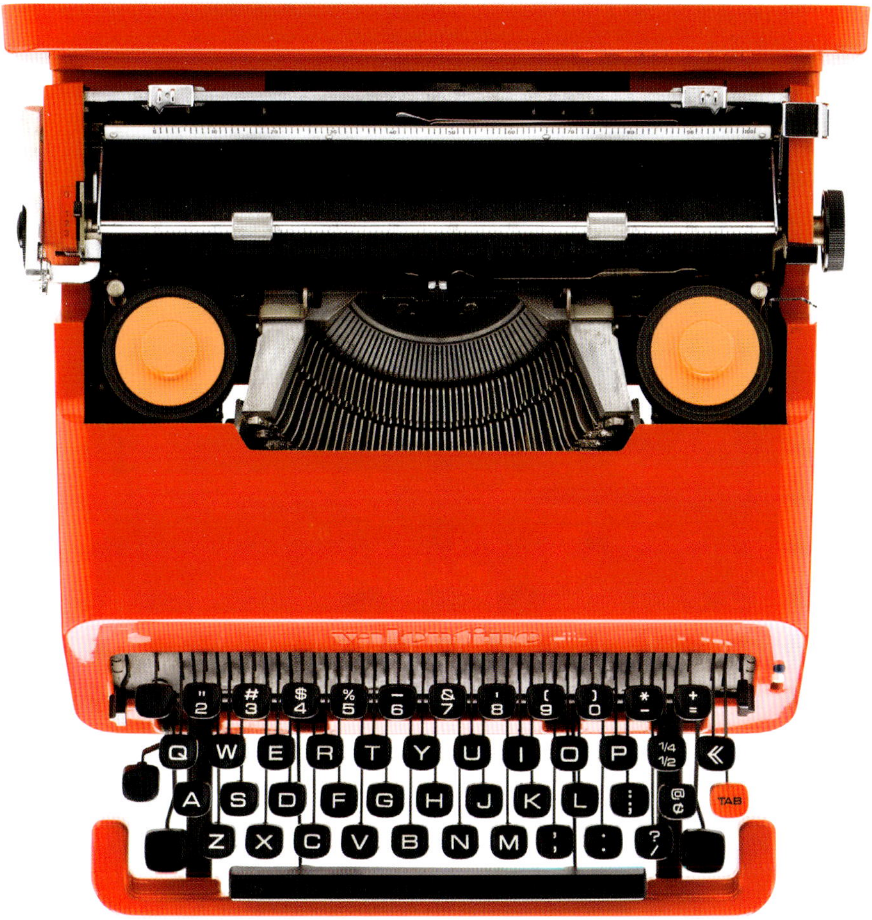
valentine

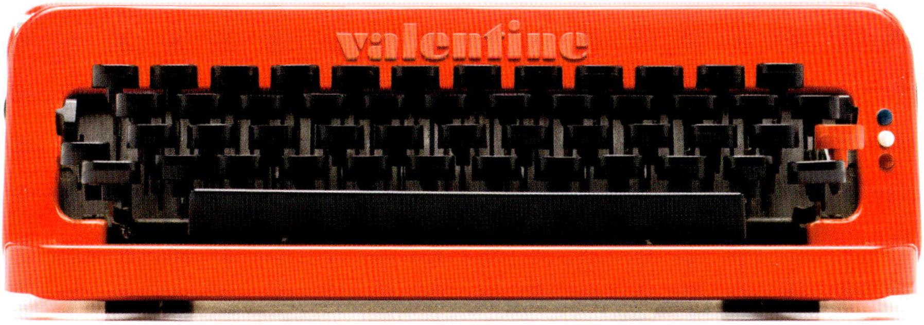
valentine

126

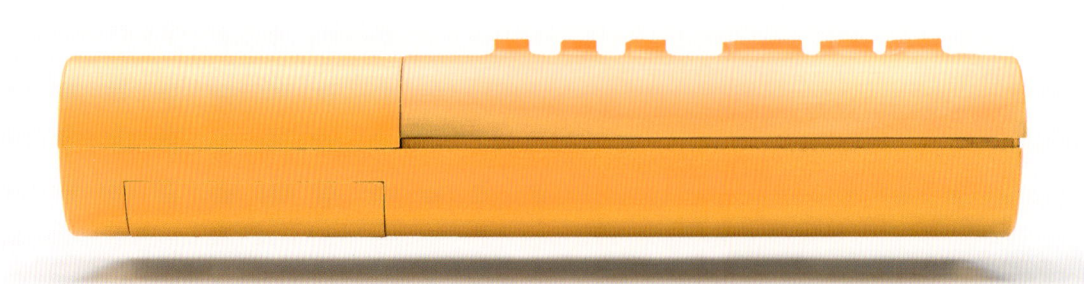

DIVISUMMA 18 PORTABLE CALCULATOR
Designed by Mario Bellini
Made by Olivetti
Italy, 1973
W: 250mm H: 50mm D: 120mm

When Mario Bellini began consulting for Olivetti in 1963 it was making the transition (within its office products division) from designing and manufacturing products that were electromechanical to ones that used microelectronic technology.

The synthetic rubber keypad of this portable calculator is soft to touch but the mechanism beneath has been designed with spring steel, which imparts a light but positive action. There is an audible click in the operation which offers confirmation. This considered approach to the tactile and expressive qualities of the materials, combined with Bellini's proclivity to include anthropomorphic elements into his products, is designed to create an emotional reaction in the user.

PLAYER
Made by Sony
Japan, 1979
W: 90mm H: 138mm D: 29mm

In developing the Walkman, Sony disregarded many features previously included in a cassette player/recorder. The Walkman had no recording capability and no speaker. The user had to wear headphones to listen to the playback.

However, the Walkman contained a circuit designed to deliver high-fidelity audio playback, it was portable and simple to operate. By reconfiguring the existing technology into an attractive, compact package, Sony brought to market an original design that proved to be an immediate commercial success internationally. Within months the Walkman was imitated by countless manufacturers.

Two features of the original Walkman were later deleted: the facility for two sets of headphones so that a program could be shared; and the hot line (orange button) which interrupted the audio and activated a microphone so the user could hear what was happening around them without removing the headphones.

A decade after the Walkman was launched a BBC documentary proclaimed: "The Japanese have a profound understanding of the principles of reductionism. It lies at the heart of their culture from Bonsai trees to rock gardens ... It is no accident that today the Japanese have surpassed the rest of the world in making intricately crafted hi-tech products."[5]

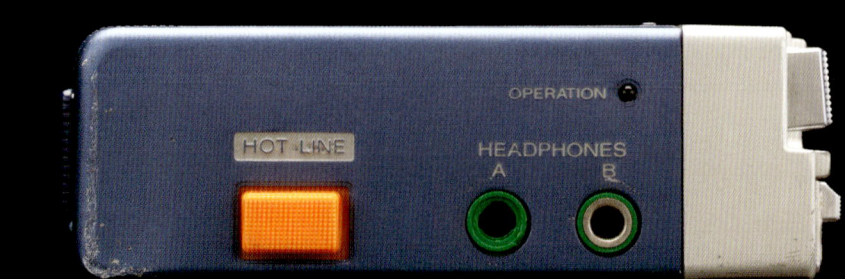

MIC
STOP
EJECT
10
5
0
LEFT
RIGHT
VOLUME
DC IN 3V
SONY
SONY
WALKMAN

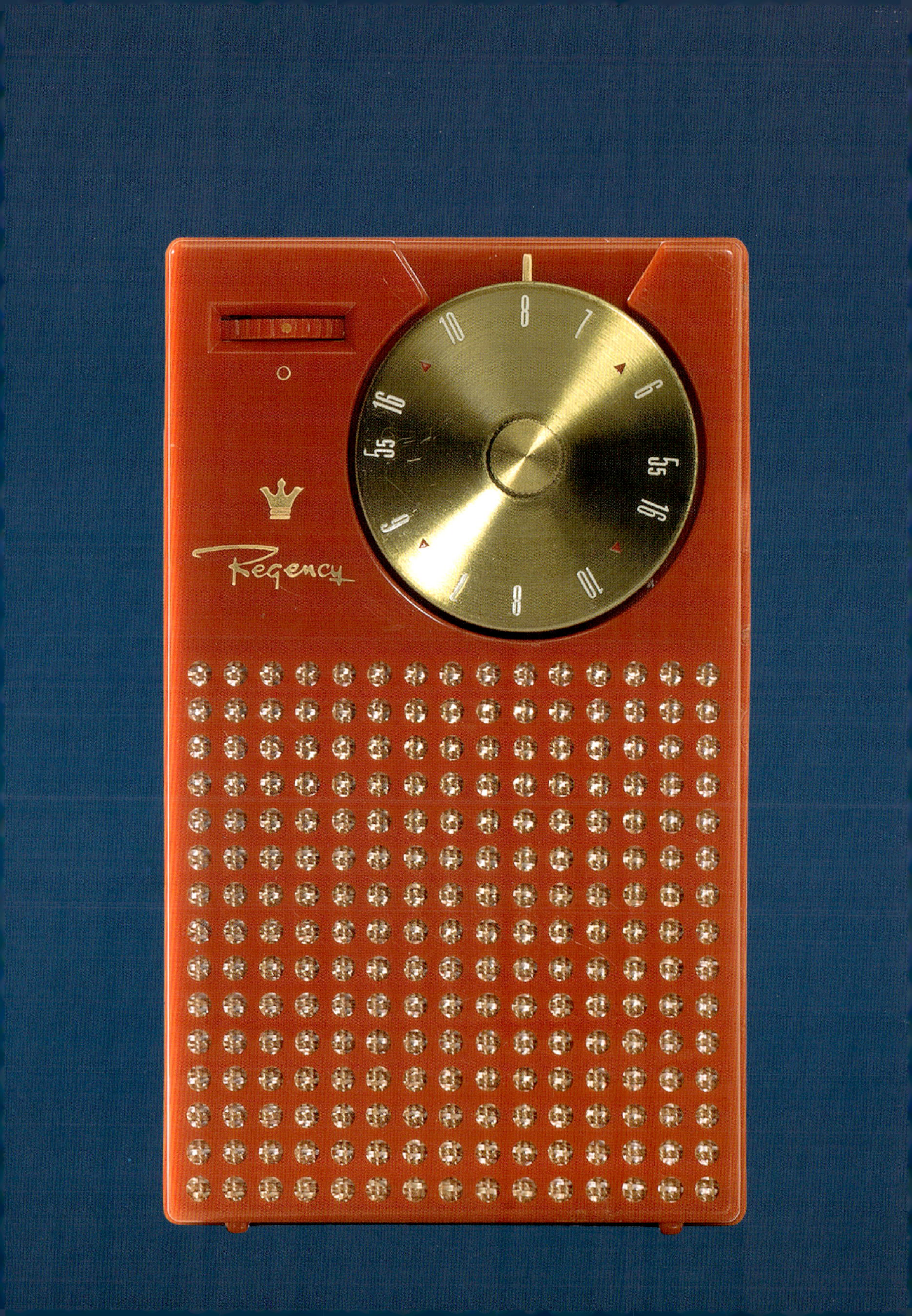
Regency

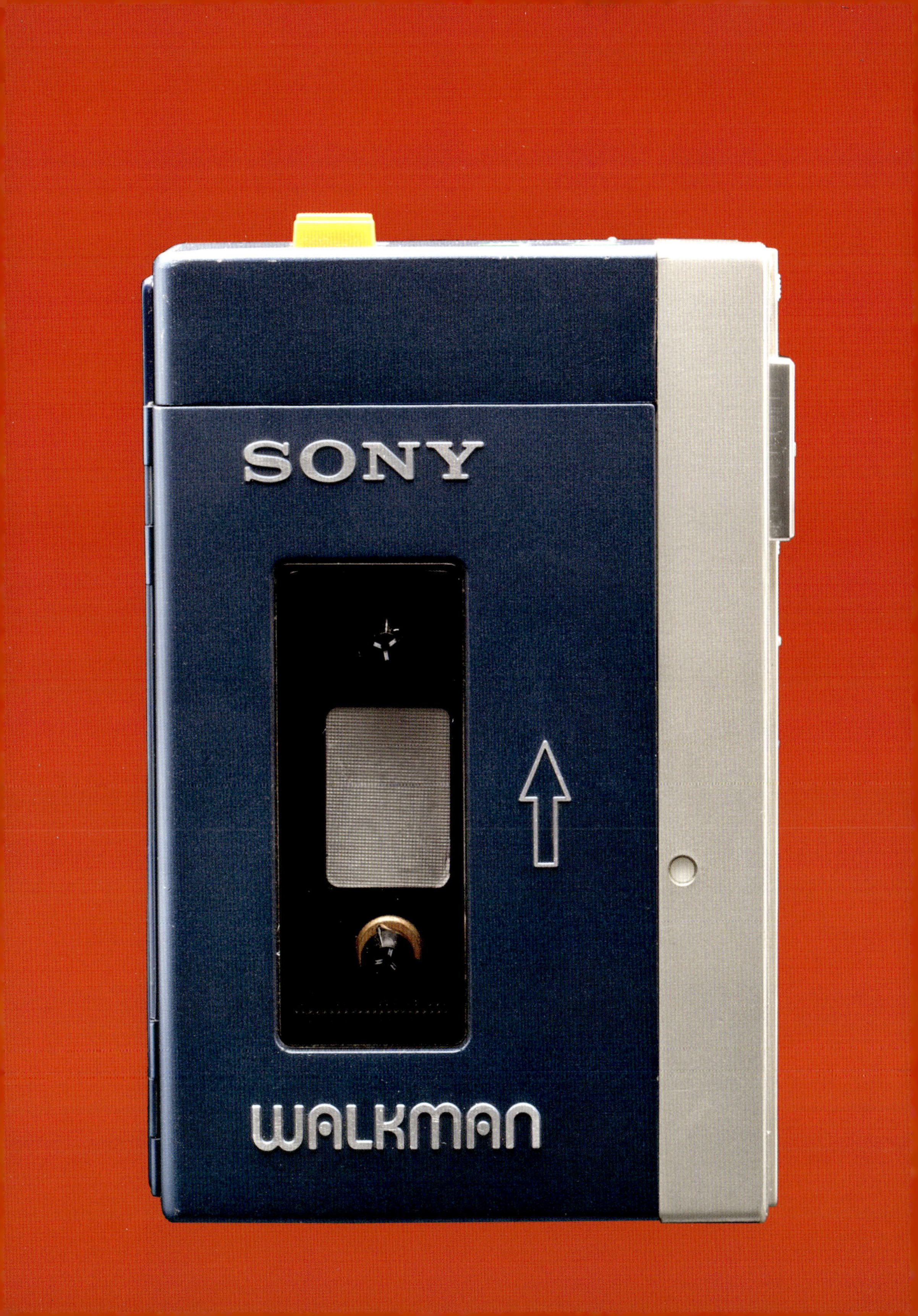
SONY
WALKMAN

TAMAGOTCHI TOY
Designed by Akihiro Yokoi of WiZ and Aki Maita of Bandai
Made by Bandai
Japan, 1996
W: 44mm H: 52mm D: 18mm

Tamagotchi is a virtual pet that requires attention and nurture to survive and mature into adult form. Users monitor the screen presence of an embryonic form that moves about and beeps to alert the carer that attention of some kind is required to maintain the creature's healthy development.

The social impact of the Tamagotchi was substantial when it was first released. School classes were disrupted by young Tamagotchi users consumed by the maintenance of their pet. The first series, of which this is one, were particularly invasive because the beeping audio could not be muted and the life cycle could not be paused, resulting in the death of the virtual pet within half a day of neglect.

Tamagotchi exposes the capacity for humans to become emotionally attached to inanimate objects, validating the design philosophy of some of the most successful designers of technological products. First released in 1996, it remains in production today.

AIBO ENTERTAINMENT ROBOT
ERS-110
Made by Sony
Japan, 1999
W: 160mm H: 266mm D: 415mm

The Aibo was Sony's first venture into domestic entertainment robots and was principally designed as a robotic companion.

Through the 1990s new toy products incorporated more compact and cheaper computer controlled technologies (including robot control software and mechanisms combined with machine intelligence programming).

The Aibo uses these technologies to develop a bond with the user. Aibo can track and interact with a coloured ball, simulating the behaviour of a real dog playing. The movement and behaviour of Aibo advance as the user spends more time interacting with it. An illusion of personality emerges from the zoomorphic characteristics and movement.

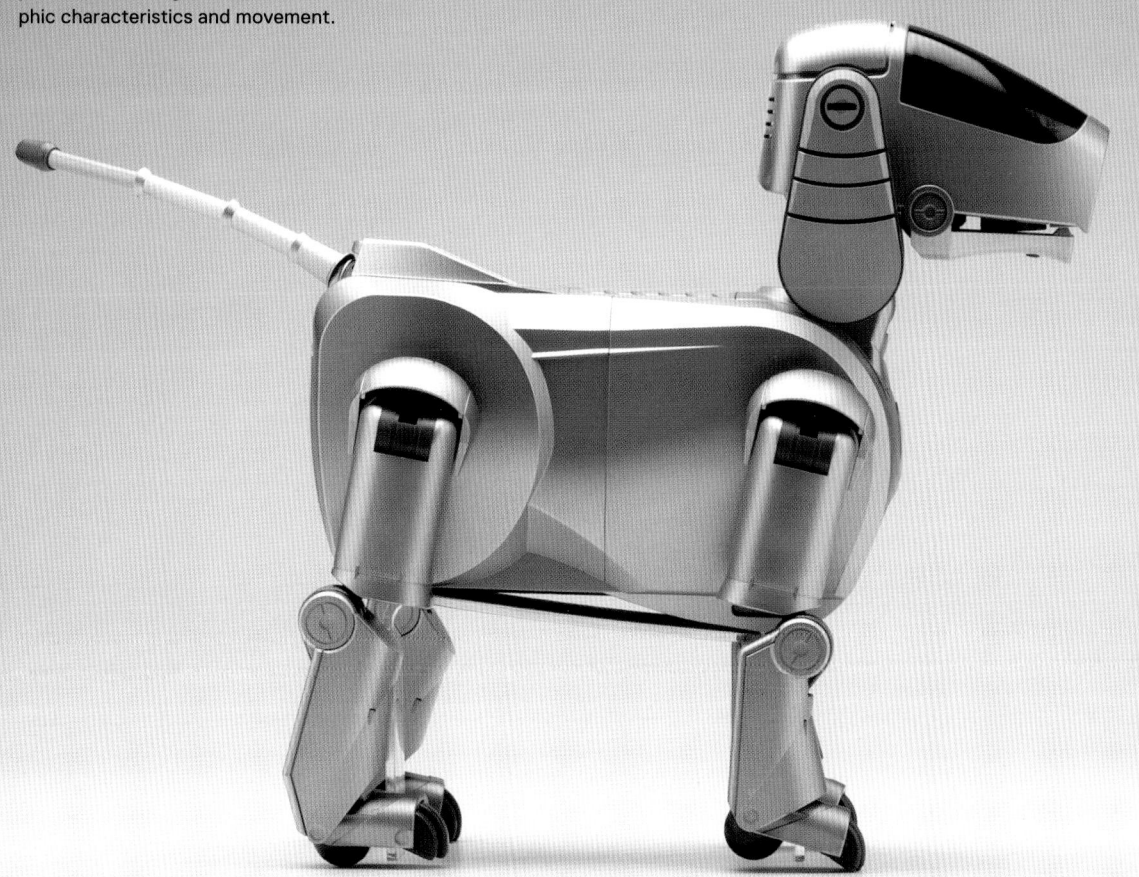

DOT MATRIX WITH STEREO SOUND
BATTERY
Nintendo GAME BOY TM
SELECT
START
B
A
PHONES

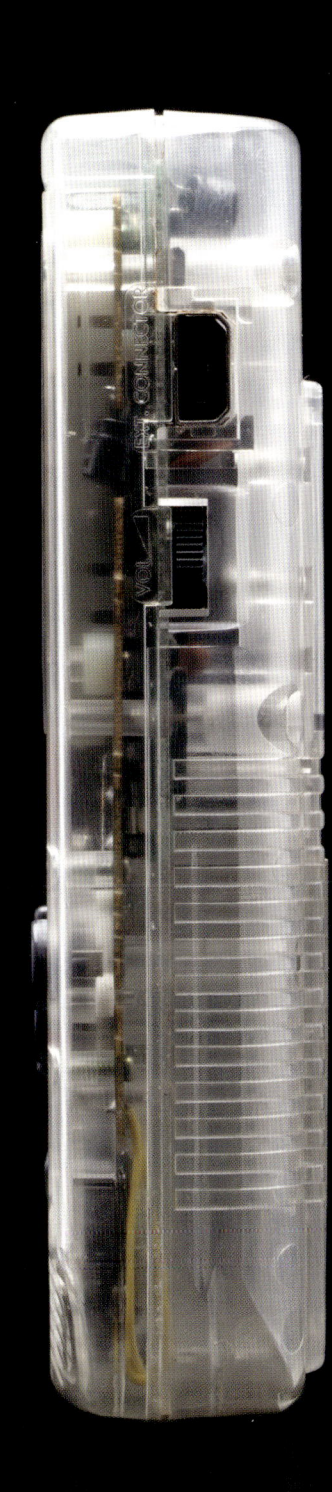

GAME BOY GAME CONSOLE
Designed by Gunpei Yokoi
Made by Nintendo
Japan, 1995
W: 88mm H: 147mm D: 33mm

The Game Boy is a hand-held electronic game console with a choice of game cartridges. This model from the 'Play it Loud' series, released in 1995, has a transparent plastic case and illustrates a trend in product design adopted in the 1990s by such companies as Alessi, Philips, Nintendo and Apple.

An incredibly popular game console, Game Boy was selling in excess of 64 million units from its inception in 1989 through to 1998 when Nintendo began production of the Game Boy colour model. It became a portable and personalised accessory in a similar way to the Sony Walkman.

Designer Gunpei Yokoi (1941–97) was employed in Nintendo's games department from the 1970s, and was responsible for some extraordinary products including the Ultrahand (an expansion arm), the Ultra Machine (a soft baseball throwing machine for the home), the Ultra Scope (a small periscope) and the Love Tester (arcade love testing). In 1981 Yokoi teamed up with Shigeru Miyamoto (who later produced Super Mario Brothers) to develop Donkey Kong.

136

LOGOS 43PD DESKTOP
CALCULATOR
Designed by Mario Bellini
Made by Olivetti
Italy, 1977
W: 265mm H: 90mm D: 250mm

Mario Bellini's 1970s work for Olivetti had an enormous impact on information technology product design in the following decade, notably at Apple. "Steve [Jobs] not only wanted our design to be the best in the computer industry, he also wanted Apple to be in the 1980s what Olivetti had been in the 1970s — an undisputed leader in industrial design," according to Apple designer Ken Campbell[6].

The Logos 43PD is a desktop calculator with a vacuum fluorescent display and printing mechanism. The mass of the calculator is separated into two distinct parts: the forward section with the keyboard; and the rear section with the printing mechanism.

BARBER'S COMB WITH SPIRIT LEVEL
Designed by Tangerine (London)
and Jonathan Ive, 1990
United Kingdom, 2010
W: 113mm H: 285mm D: 23mm

This barber's comb was designed by Jonathan Ive (1967–) a few years before he joined Apple. An example of Ive's earlier industrial design work, it demonstrates the designer's consideration of and solutions to the object's visual, haptic, ergonomic, practical and symbolic form.

The comb's lightweight construction is made possible by two plastic casing components which form a hollow rigid handle. The part lines are located at the transition from elliptical side to the low profile face, reducing the visual and physical impact of the join. The handle's graduated volume affords a comfortable grip. A spirit level within the handle indicates when the comb is being held horizontally, ensuring the perfect execution of a flat top haircut. These elements combine within this simple device for an inviting and effortless operation.

Jonathan Ive trained in industrial design and co-founded the London partnership Tangerine in 1990. He was seduced by the possibilities of designing products for Apple and joined them in 1992. Ive found a like mind with Steve Jobs' return to Apple in 1996 and they forged a partnership that steered Apple from being a computer manufacturer into a consumer electronics company that understood and applied great design.

The comb received the German Industrie Forum award in 1991.

NEWTON MESSAGEPAD 130 PERSONAL DIGITAL ASSISTANT
Designed Jonathan Ive and Apple Industrial Design
Made by Apple Computer Inc
USA, 1996
W: 100mm H: 30mm D: 200mm

The MessagePad is an electronic version (incorporating services such as email and fax) of the paper-based personal organiser. It was Jonathan Ive's first project after he joined Apple in September 1992. Ive's design was developed from initial idea to first prototype in two weeks. Although it was a rush job, to replace the original Newton MessagePad 100, Ive executed a complete rethink of the original design, making it more intuitive and appealing.

The MessagePad presents elements of Ive's playful physical designs, which seek to engage the user through an unfolding narrative of the product's features and use. It conveniently retains the handwritten element of its pre-electronic predecessor. Ive explained that as he studied the form he "discovered that by allowing the user to fiddle with the retractable pen and play with the popup lid, we could elicit the more abstract emotions of intrigue and surprise that would make Lindy (the project name for MessagePad) seem personal and precious". [7]

The Newton program had been ambitious and the products struggled in the marketplace. The later development of the iPhone conceivably benefitted from the portable computing work undertaken during the Newton development era (1987–98).

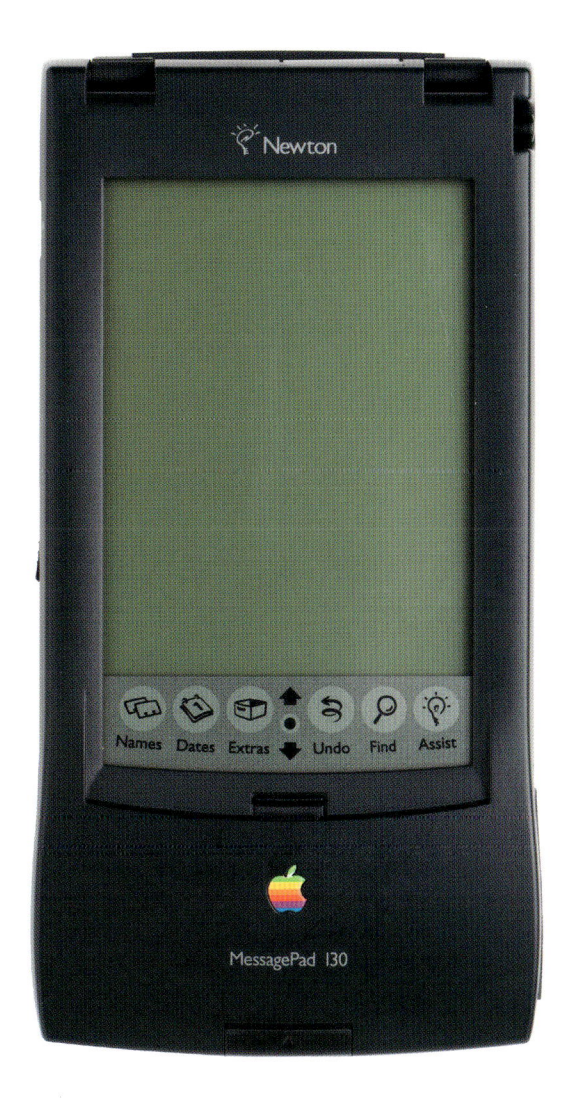

IMAC G3 BONDI BLUE
Designed by Jonathan Ive
Made by Apple Computer Inc
USA, 1998
W: 386mm H: 401mm D: 447mm

After his return to Apple in 1996, Steve Jobs chose a design that Jonathan Ive was working on to develop as a prototype for a new Apple product. The result was the iMac G3 Bondi Blue, which is credited as the Mac that saved Apple. It sold to both established Apple users and generated tremendous business with new users.

Among the computer's innovative features is the incorporation of a digital media drive and a modem to plug straight into an internet connection. It was also the first computer to eliminate the 3.25 inch floppy drive, replacing it with the facility to connect to external devices. Other manufacturers quickly followed this lead.

The Bondi Blue's other outstanding features are its form and colour. At a time when nearly all other computer makers were producing beige boxes, the iMac computer and screen was housed in one cone-shaped translucent plastic housing with a handle on the top.

Ive commented: "The iMac isn't about candy-coloured computers. The iMac is about making a computer that is really quiet, that doesn't need a fan, that wakes up in fifteen seconds, that has the best sound system in a consumer computer, a superfine display. It's about a complete computer that expresses it on the outside as well."[8]

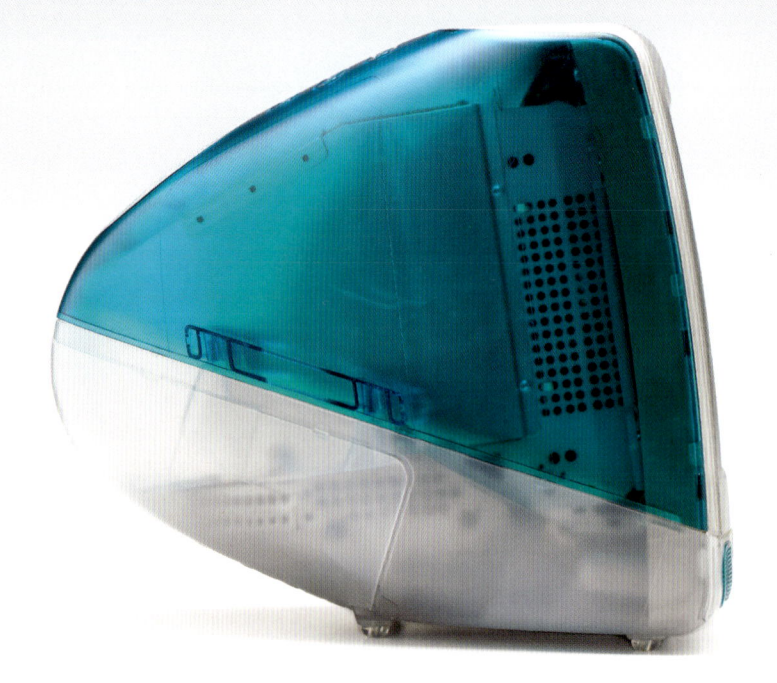

141

STUDIO DISPLAY
Designed by Jonathan Ive
Made by Apple Computer Inc
USA, 2000
W: 432mm H: 475mm D: 442mm

The 17 inch (432mm) Studio display was one of the largest and heaviest displays to come from Apple and was the last stand-alone cathode ray tube (CRT) display manufactured by the company. Weighing around five times as much as its flat screen peers and using twice as much power, it was not popular and was deleted from Apple's inventory within a year of release.

Despite these shortcomings it presents a pleasing form. The elegant converging lines visually diminish its vast physical volume and the clear acrylic case reveals all the internal components.

The clear casing, also applied to Apple audio, keyboard and mouse accessories at this time, offers the last glimpse into the mechanism of a CRT. Ive took great care in the arrangement of the internal components. The mechanism floats clear of the housing within the cavity of the case.

143

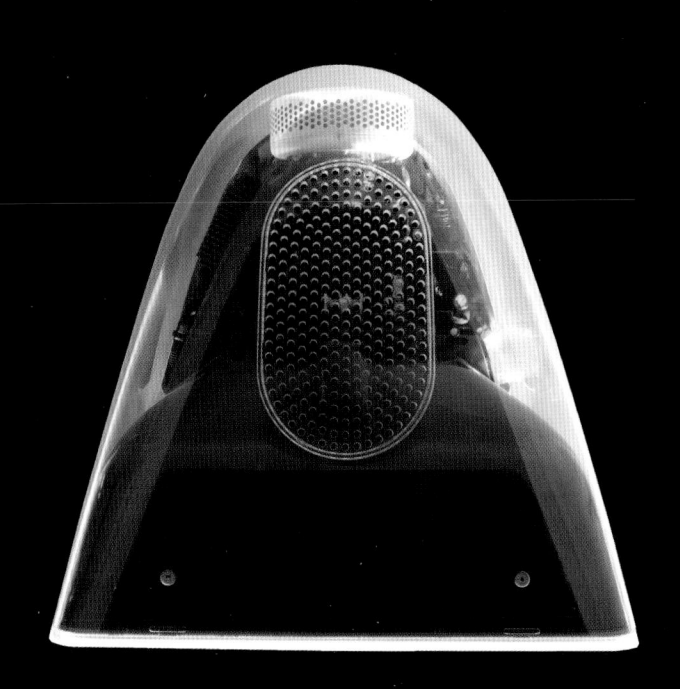

POWER MAC G4 CUBE COMPUTER
Designed by Jonathan Ive
Made by Apple Computer Inc
USA, 1999–2000
178 mm x 178 mm x 178 mm

The Power Mac G4 reduced the footprint of Apple's most powerful desktop computer to a 7 inch (178 mm) cube. It may have been a homage to the NeXT cube (305 mm) designed by Hartmut Esslinger. However, it more closely follows Ive's earlier experiments in clear and translucent plastics. It also exhibits qualities of earlier 20th century designs by Dieter Rams (for Braun), using a pale palette and simple form. A graphite-coloured plastic cube with a Lucite support holds the central processing unit.

The Cube cost around 10% more than other top-of-the-line Apple products. Sales were slow and the Cube was "put on ice" (Apple press release) after remaining in production for just a year. Despite this the Cube can be viewed as a turning point in Ive's designs for Apple products.

145

T3 TRANSISTOR RADIO
Designed by Dieter Rams in collaboration with Hochschule für Gestaltung (Ulm) School of Design
Made by Braun, Germany, 1958
W: 82mm H: 150mm D: 41mm

The T3 transistor radio was Braun's first pocket transistor radio and offers a clear illustration of Dieter Rams '10 elements of good design' principles at work. He believed that good design should make a product useful and understandable and that it should be innovative, aesthetic, unobtrusive, honest, long-lasting, thorough down to the last detail, environmentally friendly, and lastly, be as little design as possible.

The glacial style of the T3 is typical of the Braun product range that Rams designed, including the SK4 radiogram (Snow White's coffin) and the Braun RT20 radio. Braun products demonstrated the importance of good design without compromise. They were technically superior to competitors and this was reflected in their purchase price. Braun's owners (Artur and Erwin Braun) had to demonstrate considerable faith and patience in this philosophy before market acceptance rewarded it.

RIO PMP300 DIGITAL MEDIA PLAYER
Made by Diamond Multimedia Systems, Inc
USA, 1998
W: 66mm H: 92mm D: 20mm

The Diamond Rio was one of the earliest portable digital media devices. Released in late 1998, it was used for downloading and playback of MP3 files. It sold extremely well and established the MP3 file format. So much so that some sections of the record industry attempted to sue Diamond claiming the PMP300 encouraged music piracy.

The MP3 file format first appeared in the early 1990s and was rapidly gaining popularity on the internet through legitimate digital music distribution sites, closely followed by illegitimate peer-to-peer music swap sites such as Napster.

Apple executives examined the Diamond Rio when they were considering a foray into the digital media player market, although they were quick to fault its lack of user friendliness and capacity.

IPOD DIGITAL MEDIA PLAYER
Designed by Jonathan Ive
Made by Apple Computer Inc
USA, 2001
W: 62mm H: 102mm D: 20mm

A digital media player that integrated with a desktop computer application and an internet service (iTunes), the iPod quickly became the top selling device of its kind when it was released in 2001. By 2008 Apple's iPod classic and variations on it generated 40% of the company's total revenue, before the launch of the iPhone and iPod touch made the iPod redundant.

While there had been previous attempts to produce digital media devices, no one had produced a simple and elegant solution to the human-player interface. The controls resolve the functions of the machine into five buttons and one scroll wheel. Its distinctive white and clear acrylic form on a stainless steel back is intuitive to hold, touch and use.

The iPod accumulated social cachet as it was avidly consumed by a new wave of digital admirers. Holding up to 1000 songs, it became as much a new software device as a physical product.

Apple brought the iPod to market swiftly (within eight months of inception). It did so while the music industry was flustered over peer-to-peer music sharing services which had sprung up in the late 1990s (Napster 1999–2001). With no solution to this new music distribution system — surprising considering the music industry had previously shown great savvy at adopting digital recording, mastering and product formats (CD) in the 1980s — Apple forged a deal with record companies to join their iTunes service to distribute files for iPods.

The impact of the iPod was pervasive. Third party companies made and supplied accessories and many car manufacturers installed iPod docking mechanisms as standard features. Independent stereo manufacturers began to include iPod integration slots in their machines.

149

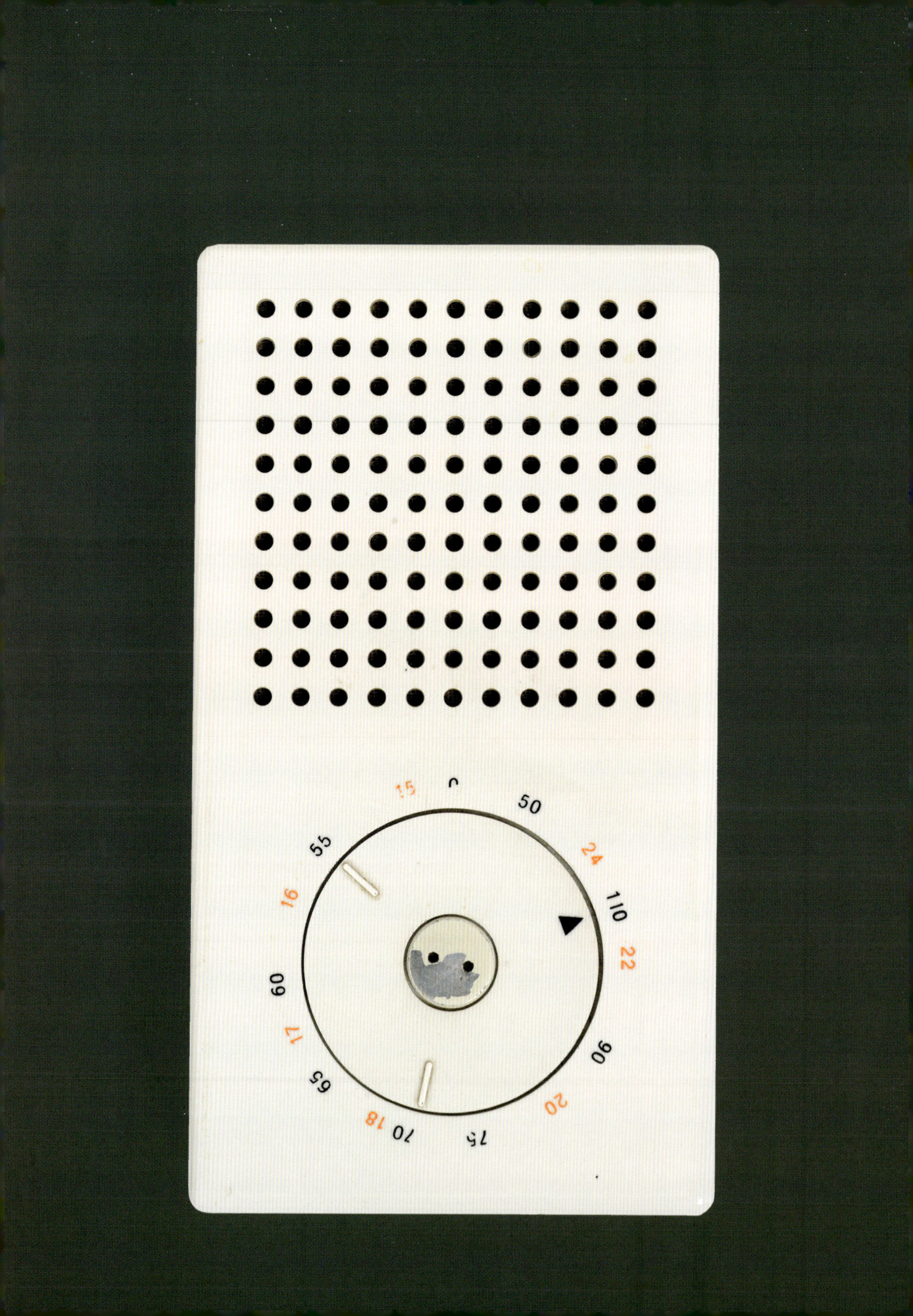
15
50
24
110
22
90
20
75
70
18
65
17
60
16
55

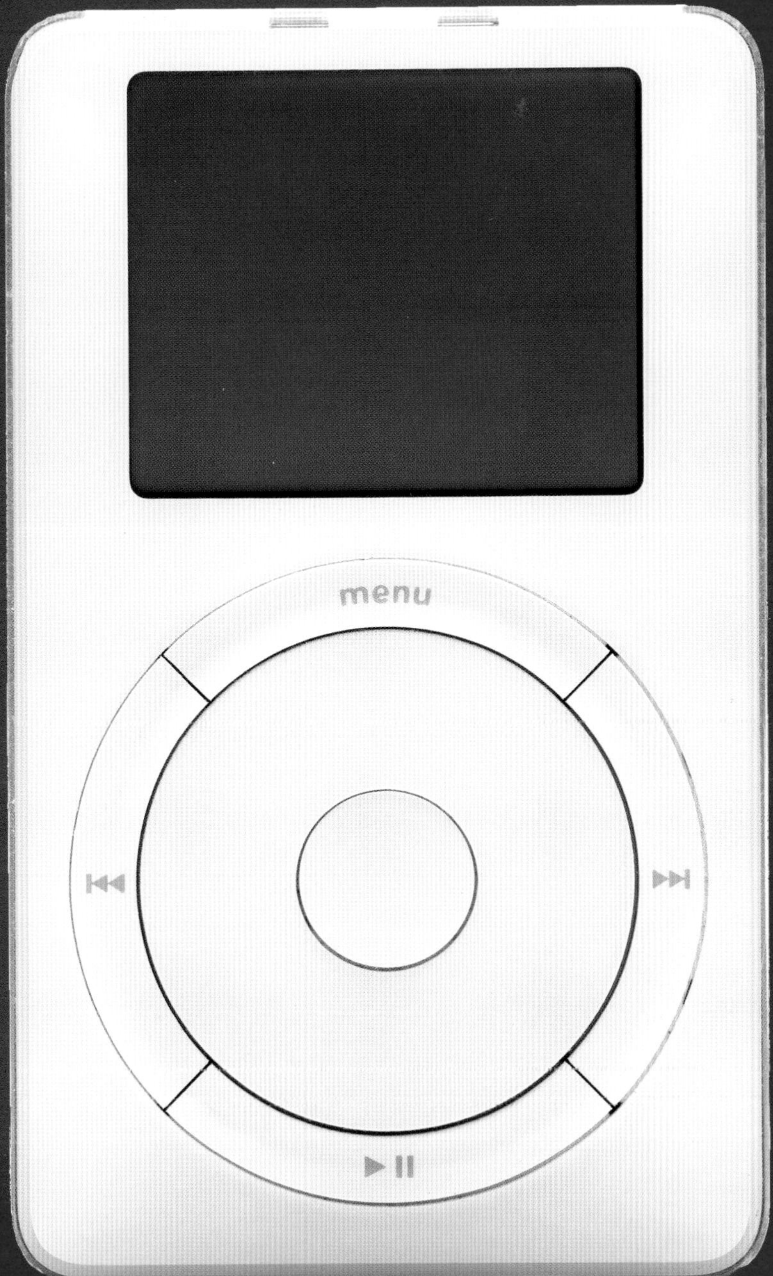
menu

POWERMAC COMPUTER
Designed by Jonathan Ive and Apple
Industrial Design group (IDg)
Made by Apple Computer Inc
USA, 2004
W: 206mm H: 511mm D: 475mm

At the time of its release the PowerMac G5 was touted as the fastest (processor speed) personal computer ever built. Around this time Apple was also implementing a strategy to reduce the environmental impact of its products through the use of highly recyclable materials, the creation of product structures that facilitated easier disassembly for recycling and the elimination of toxic chemicals used during the manufacture of various components. The G5 complied with this strategy.

Comparisons have been made between Ive's design for the Apple PowerMac G5 from 2004 and Dieter Rams' design for the Braun T1000 receiver from 1963. Both designers have expressed respect and admiration for the other's design output. Apart from a physical resemblance in form, finish, materials and treatments, there are other comparisons. Rams and Ive share a philosophy that democracy can find expression in their products. The T1000 gave radio listeners access to the world, while the iPod gave access to millions of songs and the G5 represents portability, utility, simplicity and longevity.

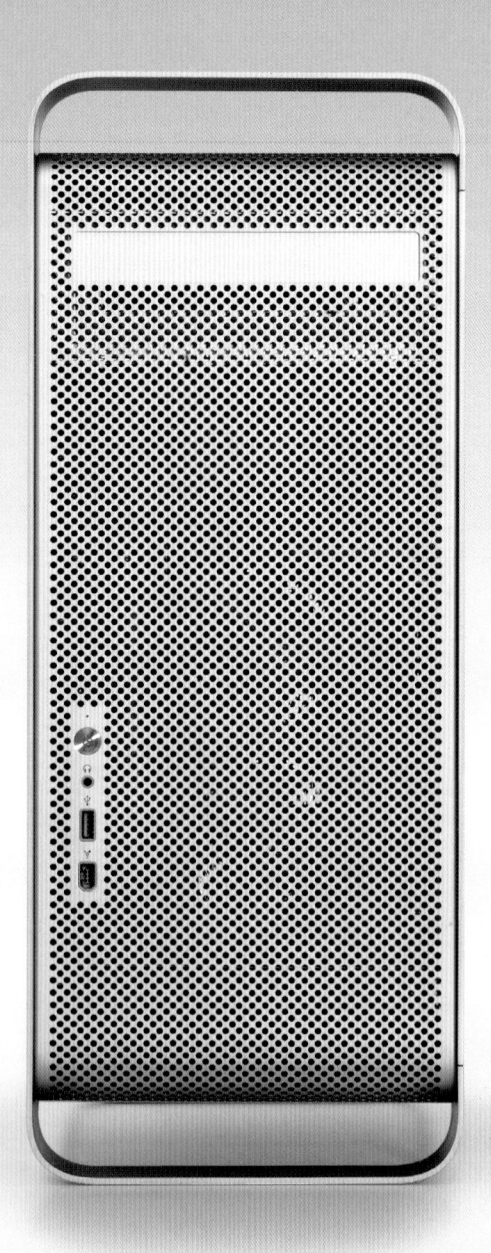

153

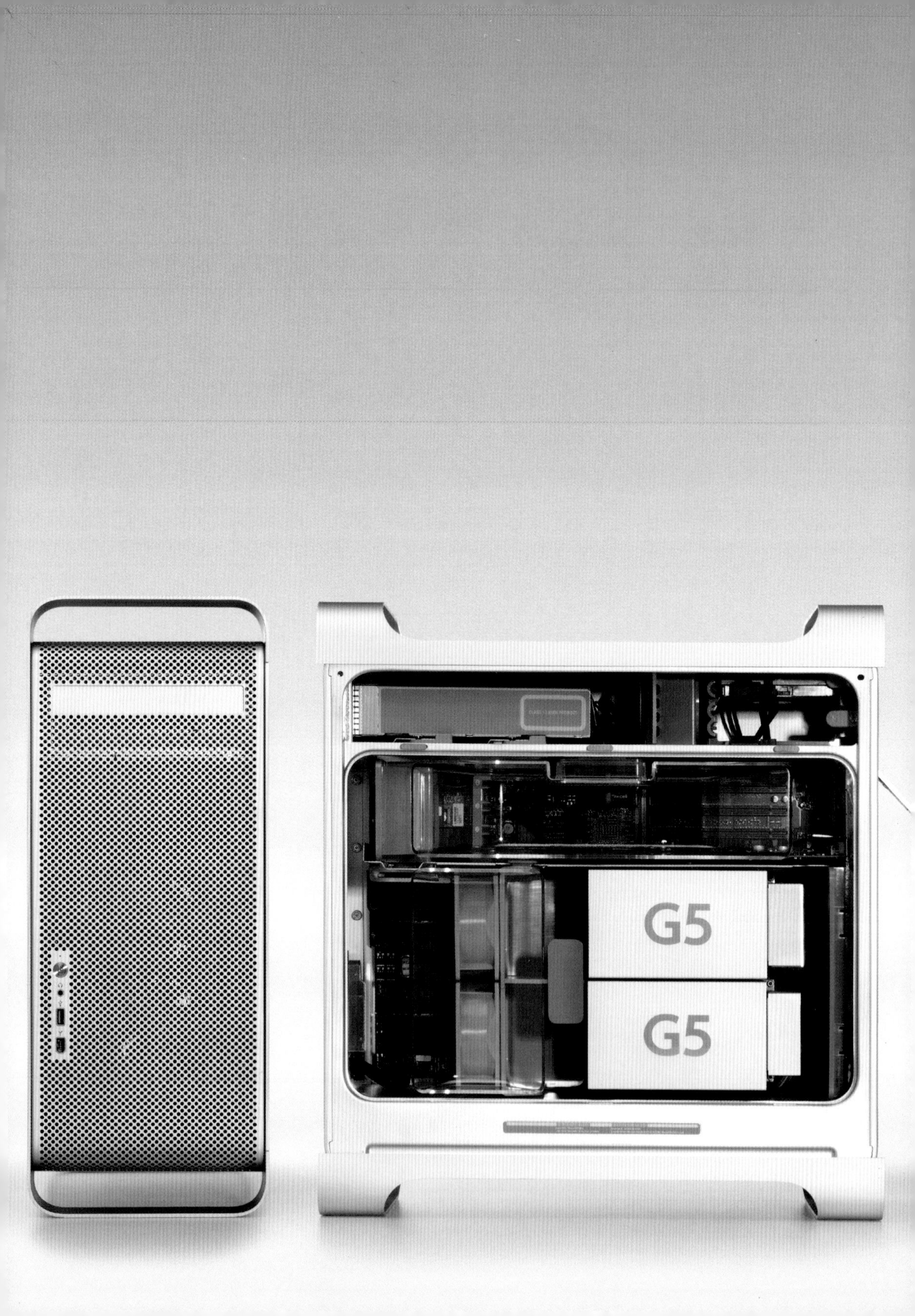
G5
G5

tuning
volume
tone
bfo
mgc
el. bandspread
off
on
line
battery
sharp
broad
dial light
on / batt. c.
afc
ferr. ant.
phono
tape
am
fm
BRAUN

156

MACBOOK PRO LAPTOP COMPUTER
Designed by Jonathan Ive
Made by Apple Inc
USA, 2010
W: 364mm H: 24mm* D: 249mm

Much of Ive's design output is dedicated to removing features or reducing the elements vying for the user's attention. His aim is a considered solution that 'speaks' to the user and reduces thoughts of 'how does this work?' People discover the product's functionality intuitively.

The design and construction of this portable personal computer employs what Apple calls the "precision aluminium unibody enclosure". The unibody was developed by Ive and the Apple Industrial Design Group and initially applied to the MacBook Air in 2008.

This most critical part (housing track pad / keyboard / drives / central processing unit) is machined from a single aluminium blank. The design of the unibody required Ive and the team to think exhaustively about the process of manufacture. The computer can be assembled with reduced time and resources and manufactured to incredibly high tolerances (fit and finish) resulting in economies of production, reduced product weight (and reduced packaging and transport costs) and a rationalisation of parts.

*Height 255mm when lid open to 90 degrees.

POWERGLOVE COMPUTER GAME ACCESSORY
Made by Mattel
China, 1989–1990
W: 180mm H: 340mm D: 80mm

The primary interface for smart phones and tablet computers is a gesture control surface. This type of interface has many predecessors, both in the real world and in science fiction.

In the late 1980s gesture control was introduced to computer games in the form of PowerGlove, an input device for the Nintendo Entertainment System. It was an alternate controller (replacing a joystick or keyboard commands) for use with games.

VPL Research Inc designed and developed the original DataGlove in the mid 1980s as a standard input device for virtual environment systems. VPL's DataGlove sold for several thousand (US) dollars. Mattel tooled down the glove's components and retailed its low-tech version for between US$70 and US$100.

The PowerGlove used analogue flex sensors embedded in the plastic on the back of the fingers to measure finger bending. Its potential was recognised by enthusiasts, hackers and virtual environment buffs.

In the 1920s Russian inventor Leon Theremin (1896–1993) demonstrated his Etherophone or Thereminovox, a musical instrument developed using radio technology and operated by gesture control. The proximity of the performer's hands to two antennas affected a circuit altering the pitch and volume of an oscillator. Theremin had observed the oscillations while developing a circuit for another experiment and refined those ideas into a musical instrument with this unique gesture control.

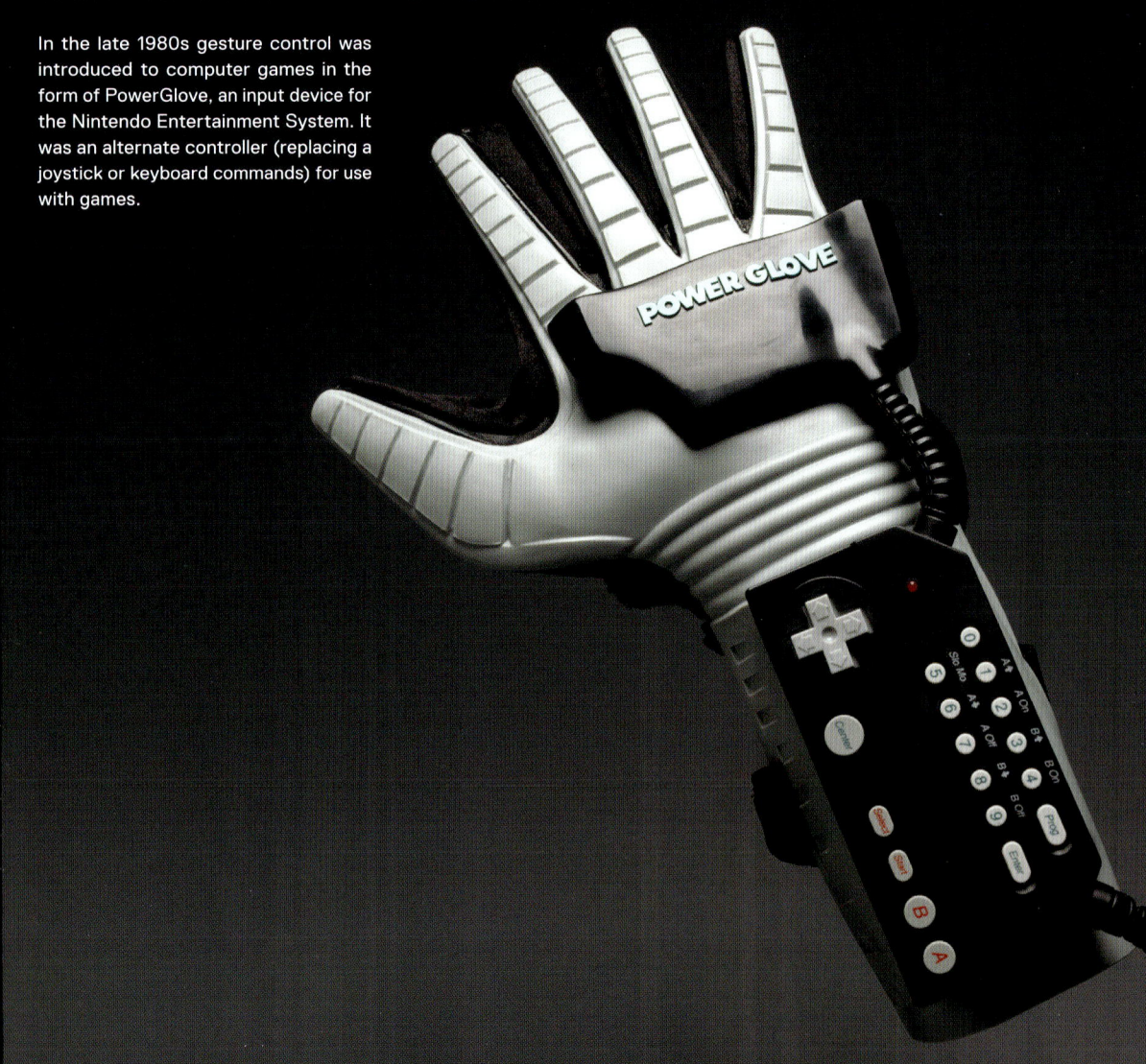

ET66 CALCULATOR
Designed by Dieter Rams and Dietrich Lubs
Made by Braun, Germany, 1987
W: 78mm H: 138mm D: 11mm

The ET66 calculator demonstrates the continuing influence of Rams' design for Braun. Most notable of all contemporary homages to Rams' designs is Jonathan Ive's recent work for Apple. The Apple iPhone calculator application (2007) was modelled directly on the Braun calculator's numeric and function keypad.

SMARTPHONE, IPHONE 2G (1ST GENERATION)
Designed by Jonathan Ive and Apple Industrial Design group (IDg)
Made by Apple Inc
USA, 2007
W: 61mm H: 115mm D: 11.6mm

The first iPhone was introduced to the North American market in June 2007 amid much hype. It was the result of a two-year collaboration between Apple and AT&T.

Apple is generally guarded about product development and strategies, however, the development of the iPhone was likely prompted by the displacement and decline of the iPod. Other manufacturers had introduced the functionality of a portable media player to their mobile phones in the years following the introduction of the iPod (2001). Apple adapted the technological developments of a touch screen to the production of a smart phone device, a move that would accelerate the redundancy of the iPod but replace it with a versatile Apple mobile product.

The iPhone has been an enormously successful product in both sales volume and recognition of its innovation. In particular, the iPhone touch screen, replacing a physical keypad with a small display, offered a greater viewable surface.

Secret agent Maxwell Smart (played by Don Adams) satirised mobile phone technology in the 1960s television series *Get Smart*. Although he worked for a super-secret organisation, Smart's shoe phone, which remained undetected by his foes, used existing technology (the rotary dial) and relied on the regular telephone service.

This image of Gordon Gekko (played by Michael Douglas) from the film *Wall Street* (1987) presents the 'uberman' — capable of influencing anybody from anywhere (the beach) while wearing anything (his pyjamas). At this time the cost of a mobile phone and service were prohibitively high, leaving their use to the ultra-powerful and rich.

SCHOOL SLATE
National School Slate Company
USA, 1900
W: 170mm H: 215mm D: 8mm

Used by Australian school students up until the mid 20th century, the slate has a black flat honed surface in a sturdy timber frame. It is light, slim and portable and can be used with chalk for writing alphabetic text, performing calculations or for free illustration. Characters and illustrations can be saved indefinitely but should the slate be required for another image or text the existing work must be erased using a wet or dry cloth. This can be done ad infinitum.

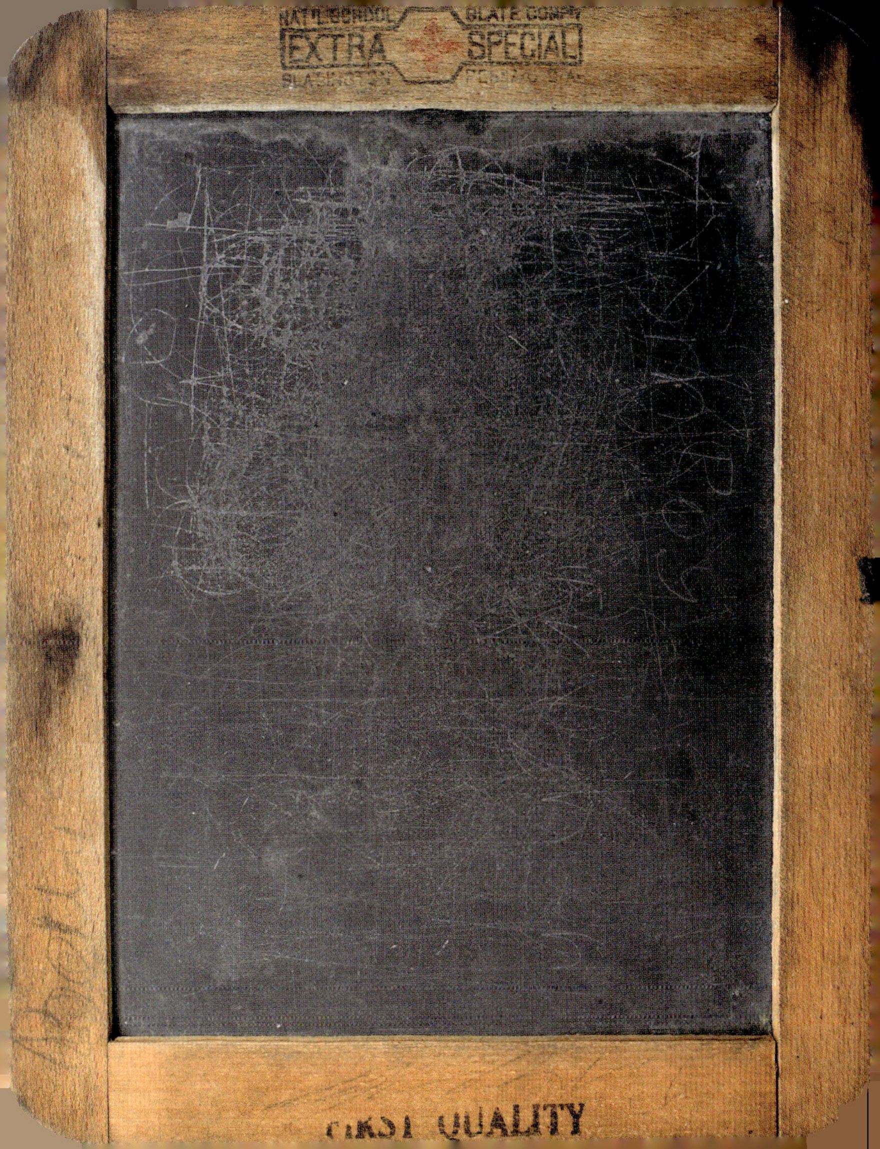
NAT'L SCHOOL
SLATE COMP'Y
EXTRA
SPECIAL
QUALITY

IPAD TABLET COMPUTER
Designed by Jonathan Ive
Made by Apple Inc
USA, 2010
W: 190mm H: 242mm D: 13.4mm

The iPad demonstrates the vision of Apple and its designers in developing a new class of device. Its intuitive interface, portability and wifi access has changed the way many people get their online information.

The iPhone and iPad development conceivably benefitted from the portable computing work undertaken during the Newton era (1987–98).

The iPad was designed by Jonathan Ive, Senior Vice President of Design at Apple Inc since 1997. He has the overall responsibility for Industrial Design and also provides leadership and direction for Human Interface (HI) software teams across the company. In 2012 he was knighted for "services to design and enterprise".

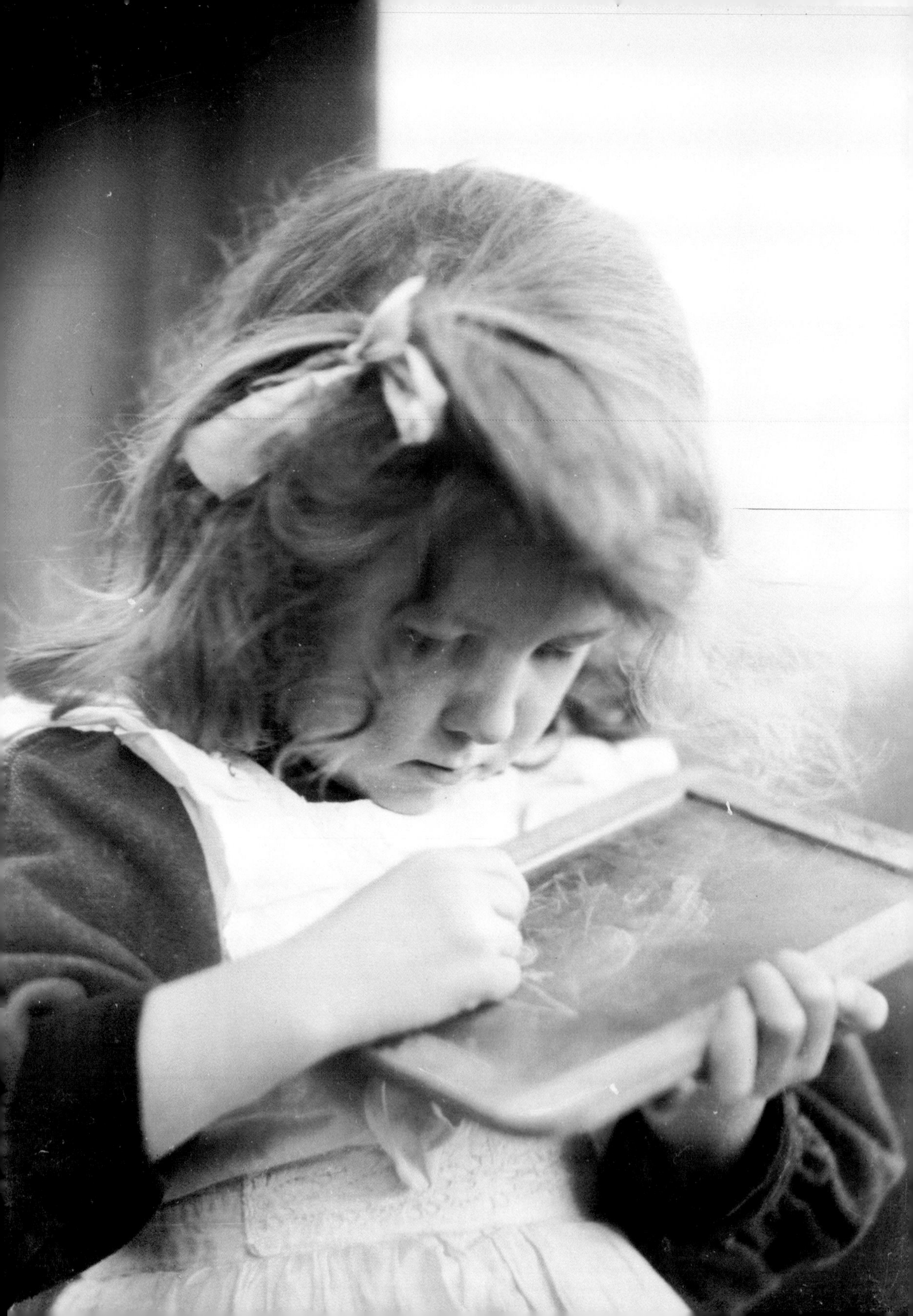

Steve Jobs with the iPad, the last product released by Apple under his leadership.

Photo of a young girl using a slate taken by Harold Cazneaux about a century earlier.

ENDNOTES

INTERFACE: PEOPLE, MACHINES, DESIGN

1. http://www.3news.co.nz/Smartphones-now-outsell-dumb phones/tabid/412/articleID/295878/Default.aspx#ixzz2pfjBopxF
2. D Liddle, 'Adopting technology' in B Moggridge, *Designing interactions*, The MIT Press, Cambridge, Massachusetts, USA, 2007, pp 242–251
3. L Burckhardt (ed), *The Werkbund: history and ideology, 1907–1933*, translated by P Sanders, Barron's, Woodbury, New York, USA, 1980; L Burckhardt, *The Werkbund*, Hyperion Press, New York, New York, USA, 1987; F J Schwartz, *The Werkbund: design theory and mass culture before the First World War*. Yale University Press, New Haven, Conneticut, USA, 1996
4. Unattributed quote believed to be Adriano Olivetti from http://storiaolivetti.telecomitalia.it
5. Of post-World War II Germany Dieter Rams said "the only thing that we had in our mind was to clean up the disturbed world . . . thinking about new designs in a clear honest way can also help democracy", quoted in 'Episode 4 Better living through chemistry', *The genius of design*, 2010, BBC2. These ideas may also have been extrapolated from lecturers and students at the Ulm School of Design who received funding from the Marshall Plan, which sought to aid the recovery of Europe.
6. Jobs' views were aligned with venture capitalist Mike Markkula's in setting up Apple. "He emphasised that you should never start a company with the goal of getting rich. Your goal should be making something you believe in and in making a company that will last." Jobs quoted in W Isaacson, *Steve Jobs*, Little, Brown, USA, 2011, p 78
7. Liddle, *op cit*, pp242-251
8. K Yasuoka and M Yasuoka, 'On the prehistory of QWERTY', *ZINBUN*, No 42 (March 2011), 2011, pp 161–174
9. Liddle, op cit, pp 242–251
10. United States patent 3541541 A, 21 June 1967
11. The GUI substituted symbols of objects for commands. 'Ornamental' design cues representing the old media, or skeuomorphs, have been used by designers to make new iterations of products familiar; the sound of a shutter on a digital camera, for example.
12. A Kay, PhD thesis, Dynabook, 1968
13. "It was like a veil being lifted from my eyes, I could see what the future of computing was destined to be." Jobs quoted in Isaacson, op cit, p 97
14. J M Carroll, 'Human computer interaction – brief intro' in Soegaard, Mads and Dam, Rikke Friis (eds), *The encyclopedia of human-computer interaction*, 2nd Ed, Aarhus, Denmark: The Interaction Design Foundation, 2013. Available online at http://www.interactiondesign.org/encyclopedia/human_computer_interaction_hci.html
15. Esslinger believed 'form follows function' a "simplistic and misunderstood reduction of Sullivan's wider description", quoted in M van Hout, 'Getting emotional with… Hartmut Esslinger', http://www.design-emotion.com, 15 August 2006
16. Isaacson, op cit, p 97
17. H Esslinger, *Keep it simple: the early design years of Apple*, Arnoldsche Art Publishers, Stuttgart, Germany, 2013
18. Jonathan Ive quoted in P Kunkel, *Apple design: the work of the Apple Industrial Design group*, Graphis Inc, New York, New York, USA, 1997, p 255
19. Quoted in G Hustwit, *Objectified: a documentary film by Gary Hustwit*, 2009
20. Carroll, *op cit*
21. The quote "We shape our tools and then our tools shape us" was in fact written by Father John Culkin, SJ, Professor of Communication at Fordham University, New York, who sought to express an idea of McLuhan's, in J M Culkin, 'A schoolman's guide to Marshall McLuhan' *Saturday Review*, 18 March 1967, pp 51–53, 71–72.

THE THINKING MAN'S FOOD PROCESSOR: DOMESTICITY, GENDER, AND THE APPLE II

1. This is an amended excerpt of J A Stein, 'In memoriam: Domesticity, gender and the 1977 Apple II personal computer', *Design and Culture*, vol 3, no 2, July 2011, pp 193–216, published by Berg, an imprint of Bloomsbury.
2. P Atkinson, 'The (in) difference engine: Explaining the disappearance of diversity in the design of the personal computer', *Journal of Design History*, vol 13, no 1, 2000, pp 67–70
3. J Webster, 'From the word processor to the micro: gender issues in the development of information technology in the office', in E Green, J Owen & D Pain (eds), *Gendered by design? Information technology and office systems*, Taylor & Francis, London and Washington DC, 1993, pp 119–20. See also: C Cockburn 'The circuit of technology: Gender, identity and power', in R Silverstone, and Hirsch, Eric (ed), *Consuming technologies: Media and information in domestic spaces*, Routledge, London and New York, 1992, pp 32–47; and J Wajcman 'The feminisation of work in the information age', in D G Johnson & J M Wetmore (eds), *Technology and society: Building our sociotechnical future*, MIT Press, London and Cambridge, Massachusetts, 2009 [2006], pp 459–74
4. Apple later manufactured computer monitors to accompany their Apple II computers, but in the first release in April 1977, users were expected to provide their own televisual monitors, as was common practice in the microcomputer industry at the time.
5. Apple Computer advertisement *Byte*, August 1978, pp 14–15
6. R Silverstone, E Hirsch, D Morley, 'Information and communication technologies and the moral economy of the household', in Silverstone and Hirsch (eds), *Consuming technologies: Media and information in domestic spaces*, Routledge, London and New York, 1992, p 19
7. For detailed analysis of the various influences on computer design form, see: P Atkinson, 'Computer memories:

FAN FRICTION:
DESIGN-CENTRIC
BATTLE LINES IN THE
SMART PHONE AGE

The history of computer form', *History and Technology*, vol 15, no 1/2, 1998, pp 1–32; Atkinson, *Computer*, Reaktion Books, New York, 2010; Atkinson, 'Man in a briefcase: The social construction of the laptop computer and the emergence of a type form', *Journal of Design History*, vol 18, no 2, 2005, pp 191–205

8   The organised, bureaucratic aesthetic of IBM, and its engagement with modern design, is discussed in nuanced ways in R Martin, *The organisational complex: Architecture, media, and corporate space*, MIT Press, Cambridge, Massachusetts, 2003, pp 168–81

9   O Linzmayer, *Apple confidential 2.0: The definitive history of the world's most colourful company*, No Starch Press, San Francisco, 2004, p 14

10 Atkinson, *Computer*, p 88

11 L Kahney, *Inside Steve's brain*, Portfolio, New York, 2008, pp 73–74

12 P Kunkel, *Apple design: The work of the Apple Industrial Design group*, Watson-Guptill Publications, New York, 1997, p 13

13 Atkinson, *op cit*, p 88

14 Kahney, *op cit*, p 74

15 Jerry Manock had previously worked at Hewlett-Packard, designing calculator cases.

16 Kahney, *op cit*, p 74

17 Linzmayer, *op cit*, p 13, Kahney, *op cit*, pp 73–75

18 Kahney, *op cit*, p 75

19 Kunkel, *op cit*, p 13

20 *Byte* was an American microcomputing magazine, published from 1975 to 1998.

21 It is possible that his papers are the Apple *BASIC* manual of computer commands.

22 Webster, *op cit*, p 119

23 1983: when Apple released its first computer with a mouse, the Lisa.

24 Atkinson, 'The (in)difference engine', pp 68–69; Atkinson, 'The best laid plans of mice and men: The computer mouse in the history of computing', *Design Issues*, vol 23, no 3, 2007, p 59

1   http://www.cnet.com.au/marc-newson-on-iphone-god-is-in-the-detail-339341712.htm

2   http://www.themodernword.com/eco/eco_mac_vs_pc.html

3   Apple Think Different advertising campaign, television commercial script, 1998.

4   http://www.t3.com/news/smart phones-are-the-latest-fashion-accessory-says-blackberry-head

5   http://www.t3.com/news/smart phones-need-more-style-than-substance-says-samsung

6   http://www.theguardian.com/technology/2007/oct/27/gadgets.digitalmedia

7   http://www.scribd.com/doc/43945579/Playboy-Interview-With-Steve-Jobs

8   http://daringfireball.net/2013/12/lightning_apple

9   http://www.isuppli.com/Teardowns/News/Pages/Groundbreaking-iPhone5s-Carries-199-BOM-and-Manufacturing-Cost-IHS-Teardown-Reveals.aspx

10 A Lashinsky, *Inside Apple*, John Murray Publishers, 2012, p 49

ENDNOTES

THE ENTHUSIASTS
WE SHAPE OUR TOOLS

1. C Dresser, *Studies in design*, Gibbs Smith, England, 1874
2. T Buddensieg, 'Industriekultur Peter Behrens and the AEG, 1907-1914', In T Buddensieg (ed), Industrie-kultur, Gebr, Mann Verlag, Berlin, p14
3. R Messenger, *100 years of Olivetti typewriters: Adriano the aesthete*, self published, 2011
4. S Wozniak, 'The making of an engineer and a computer', *The Computer Museum Report*, Vol 17 Fall 1986, p 8
5. Wozniak, *ibid*, p 7

THE PROFESSIONALS
FROM USABILITY TO SOCIABILITY

1. Professional Computer System, *IEEE Annals*, Vol 28 # 4, 1985
2. Arthur C Clarke quoted in interview, 2001, http://hp9100.com/
3. Terry Oyama quoted in P Kunkel, *Apple design: the work of the Apple industrial design group*, Graphis Inc, New York, 1997, p 26
4. Anthony Guido quoted in Kunkel, *ibid*, p 54;
5. Stephen Peart quoted in Kunkel, *ibid*, p 43
6. T Berners-Lee, *Weaving the web*, Harper Collins, New York, 1998 p 28
7. R Standefer, 'Evolution of Mac OS X', *Macintosh switcher's guide*, Wordware Publishing, 2004, p 33

THE CONSUMERS
FORM FOLLOWS EMOTION

1. R Handy, M Erbe, A Antonier, *Made in Japan, transistor radios of the 1950s and 1960s*, Chronicle Books, San Francisco, 1993
2. K Klemp (ed), *Less and more the design ethos of Dieter Rams*, Verlag: Die Gestlten Verlag GmbH & Co, KG Berlin, Germany, 2011, p 483
3. D Cowley and J Pavitt (eds), *Cold War modern design 1945–1970*, London, 2008, p 1
4. A Castiglioni, *Alla Castiglioni*, Cosmit, 1996; P Antonelli, S Guarnaccia, *Achille Castiglioni*, Corraini, 2001; S Polano, *Achille Castiglioni: complete works*, Electa, 2002
5. 'Sony Walkman', Design Classics, BBC, UK, 1990
6. Ken Campbell quoted in Kunkel, *op cit*, p 28
7. Kunkel, *op cit*, p 255
8. Jonathan Ive quoted in S Levy, *The perfect thing*, Simon and Shuster, 2006, p 95–96

PHOTO CREDITS

ALL OBJECT PHOTOGRAPHS BY MUSEUM OF APPLIED ARTS AND SCIENCES UNLESS OTHERWISE STATED.

P7	Woman with TE300 teleprinter in *Olivetti concept and form*, 1970, courtesy Associazione Archivio Storico Olivetti, Ivrea, Italy
P9	Adriano Olivetti portrait, courtesy Associazione Archivio Storico Olivetti, Ivrea, Italy
P9	Erwin and Artur Braun portrait, copyright Braun GmbH, Kronberg
P9	Steve Jobs and Steve Wozniak portrait, 1976, courtesy Apple Inc
P12	Scene from *The Day the Earth Stood Still*, 1951, courtesy Snapper Media
P14	*Les ouvriers sur la charrette*, 1914. © Alberto Magnelli /ADAGP. Licensed by Viscopy, 2014. © Centre Pompidou, MNAM-CCI, Dist. RMN-Grand Palais / Georges Meguerditchian
P15	Olivetti advertisement, Walter Ballmer, courtesy Associazione Archivio Storico Olivetti, Ivrea, Italy
P16	Worry beads, Richard Gulezian Photography
P19	Mario Bellini portrait, photo by Marie Letz, courtesy Mario Bellini Architects
P22	Divissuma 18, courtesy Mario Bellini Architects
P27	IBM 360 model 65 computer, courtesy of the Computer History Museum
P30	Apple II advertisement, 1977, courtesy Apple Inc
P33	People on mobile phones, Pressmaster/Shutterstock.com
P34	Mobile phone blur, Pan Xunbin/Shutterstock.com
P35	Macintosh launch, © Rue des Archives/RDA/Headpress
P49	AEG price list, 1912
P54	Olivetti advertisement, Xanti Schawinsky, courtesy Associazione Archivio Storico Olivetti, Ivrea, Italy
P58	Olivetti advertisement, Giovanni Pintori, courtesy Associazione Archivio Storico Olivetti, Ivrea, Italy
P60	Studio Marcello Nizzoli, photo by Ugo Mulas, © Eredi Mulas, Stampa su carta fotografica (vintage print) 28.7 x 23.5 cm, courtesy Collezione Francesco Moschini e Gabriel Vaduva A.A.M. Architettura Arte Moderna
P67	*Reclining figure 1976* © The Henry Moore Foundation, www.henry-moore.org/DACS. Licensed by Viscopy, 2014. Reproduced by permission of The Henry Moore Foundation
P72	Blue box, courtesy Computer History Museum
P81	P101 team portrait, courtesy Associazione Archivio Storico Olivetti, Ivrea, Italy
P82	Olivetti advertisement, Igis Stucchi, courtesy Associazione Archivio Storico Olivetti, Ivrea, Italy
P89	Mario Bellini portrait, courtesy Mario Bellini Architects
P92	Ettore Sottsass portrait, from *Ettore Sottsass* exhibition catalogue, promoted by Cosmit and organised by iSaloni spa, Salone Internazionale del Mobile, 13–18 April 1999, catalogue © Cosmit
P98	Douglas Engelbart portrait, courtesy SRI International
P99	Alto computer, courtesy PARC, a Xerox company
P102	Susan Kare portrait, courtesy Susan Kare kare.com kareprints.com
P103	Apple icons, courtesy Apple Inc
P104	Hartmut Esslinger portrait, courtesy frog design
P113	Regency transistor advertisement, courtesy James Butters, www.jamesbutters.com
P114	Dieter Rams portrait, © Braun GmbH, Kronberg
P115	Hans Gugelot portrait, courtesy Guus Gugelot
P118	*Superman*, © Roman Cieslewicz / ADAGP. Licensed by Viscopy, 2014. © ADAGP, Paris, 2014 – Cliché: Piotr Trawinski / Banque d'Images de l'ADAGP
P124	Olivetti advertisement, Milton Glaser, courtesy Associazione Archivio Storico Olivetti, Ivrea, Italy
P128	Postcard, Hangyoku with bonsai tree, 1905
P138	Jonathan Ive portrait, photo by Marcus Dawes
P158	Leo Theremin, © Spaarnestad / Rue des Archives / Headpress
P161	Don Adams, Everett Collection/Headpress
P161	Michael Douglas, 20th Century Fox/The Kobal Collection/Headpress
P166	*Jean writing on a slate*, photo by Harold Cazneaux, 1914, reproduced from the negative, National Library of Australia, vn5964171
P167	Steve Jobs portrait, Bloomberg/Getty Images

OBJECT ACKNOWLEDGMENTS

P5 — Apple 1 personal computer (circuit board detail) acquired 2010, 2010/6/1

P23 — Yamaha cassette deck, gift of Monica Gobel, 2004. 2004/113/1

P24 — Cab chair, purchased 1985, 85/1829

P40 — *Studies in Design* book, purchased 1989. 89/1588

P41 — Earthenware vase, gift of Bob Meyer under the Tax Incentives for the Arts Scheme, 1997. 97/268/1

P42 — Mechanical calculator, gift of Government Astronomer, 1950. B1131-2

P44 — 'Eiffel Tower' telephone, gift of Electrical Engineering Department, University of Technology, 1953. B1204

P47 — Blickensderfer 6 portable typewriter, purchased 2013. 2013/117/1

P48 — Electric kettle, purchased 1997. 97/152/1

P50 — *Die Form Ohne Ornament* book, purchased 1989. 89/1590

P51 — Field radio device (E 143a), gift of Department of Electrical Engineering, University of Sydney, 1959. 2004/14/1

P52 — Volksempfänger VE 301w radio, purchased 2012. 2012/9/1

P54 — Ico MP1 (Modello Portatile 1) typewriter, gift of Peter Fischer, 2012. 2012/138/1

P56 — 'Bauhaus' telephone, purchased 2013. 2013/119/1

P58 — Summa 15 calculator, purchased 2013. 2013/98/1

P60 — Lettera 22 typewriter, purchased 2013. 2013/118/1

P62 — MC24 Divisumma calculator, gift of Angus Campbell, 1981. K456

P64 — 2+7 telephone, purchased 2005. 2005/91/1

P68 — Trub telephone, purchased 2013. 2013/97/1

P70 — 8080 personal computer kit, gift of John W Haymes, 1996. 96/403/1

P72 — Blue Box, lent by Computer History Museum, California

P73 — Apple I personal computer, acquired 2010, 2010/6/1

P76 — Selectric 715 typewriter, gift of Lexmark International (Australia) Pty Ltd, 2003. 2003/76/3

P77 — Executary dictation machine, gift of Graeme Bull, 2008. 2008/131/1-3/1-1

P77 — Magnetic belt packaging, gift of Graeme Bull, 2008. 2008/131/1-1/5

P79 — 2250 display unit, source unknown, 2008. 2008/176/1-2

P80 — Programma 101 computer, gift of Faculty of Engineering, University of Sydney, 2008. 2008/107/1-1/1

P84 — HP 9100A programmable calculator (computer), gift of Hewlett Packard Australia, 1986, 86/1459-1

P86 — HP-65 calculator, gift of Hewlett-Packard Australia, 1986. 86/387-1

P88 — Lettera 35 typewriter, gift of Helen Duxbury, 2013. 2013/26/1

P90 — Logos 55 desk top calculator, purchased 2012. 2012/97/1

P92 — TES 501/55 word processor, gift of Darlinghurst Youth Resource Centre, 1989. 89/279-1

P94 — Dasher D2 computer terminal, gift of Data General Corp, 2003. 2003/37/1

P96 — Apple II computer, ex-Museum 2012/136/1

P97 — Apple II Monitor, ex-Museum 2012/136/1

P97 — Apple Disk II disk drive, gift of NSW Dept of Urban Affairs & Planning, 1997. 97/89/1-2

P98 — Computer mouse (replica), gift of Logitech, USA, care of: Logitech Australia Computer Peripherals Pty Ltd, 2007. 2007/150/1

P99 — Alto computer, lent by Computer History Museum, California

P100 — Macintosh 128 personal computer, gift of Peter Henderson, 1997. 97/174/2

P104 — Apple IIc computer, gift of Greg Martyn, 2012. 2012/39/1

P106 — ImageWriter II dot matrix printer, purchased 2012. 2012/96/1

P108 — NeXT computer central processing unit, gift of Data General, 2002. 2003/41/1-1

P112 — Transistor radio, purchased 1956. H5580-2

P114 — RT20 radio, purchased 2013. 2013/127/1

P115 — SK55 Phonosuper radiogram, purchased 1985. 85/2326

P118 — T1000 Weltempfaenger (world receiver) radio, purchased 2013. 2013/128/1

P120 — Lectron radio receiver, purchased 2013. 2013/13?/1

P122 — RR 126 stereo radiogram, gift of Belinda Franks under the Tax Incentives for the Arts Scheme, 2003. 2003/27/1

P124 — Valentine typewriter, gift of Mike Dawborn and Cathy Lambert, 2003. 2003/13/1

P126 — Divisumma 18 portable calculator, purchased 2013. 2013/100/1

P128 — Walkman audio cassette player, gift of Peter Tilley, 2003. 2003/165/1-1

P132 — Tamagotchi toy, purchased 2013. 2013/88/1

P133 — Aibo Entertainment Robot ERS-110, purchased 2000. 2000/12/1-1

P134 — Game Boy game console, purchased 2012. 2012/73/1

P136 — Logos 43PD desk top calculator, purchased 2012. 2012/92/1

P138 — Barber's comb with spirit level, purchased 2013. 2013/89/1

P139 — Newton MessagePad 130 personal digital assistant, purchased 2013. 2013/116/1

P140 — iMac G3 Bondi Blue, gift of John Deane, Australian Computer Museum Society, 2013. 2014/1/1

P142 — Studio display, gift of Damian McDonald, 2012. 2012/94/1

P144 — Power Mac G4 Cube computer, gift of Jones Architecture, 2013. 2013/39/1

P146 — T3 transistor radio, purchased 2012. 2012/30/1

P147 — Rio PMP300 digital media player, purchased 2012. 2012/32/1

P148 — iPod 5Gb digital media player, purchased, 2013. 2013/101/1

P152 — PowerMac G5 computer, ex-Museum, 2013. 2013/102/1

P156 — MacBook Pro 15" laptop computer, ex-Museum, 2013. 2013/96/1

P158 — PowerGlove computer game accessory, purchased 1999. 99/38/1-1

P159 — ET66 calculator, purchased 2012. 2012/33/1-1

P160 — Smartphone, iPhone 2G (1st generation), purchased 2013. 2013/124/1

P162 — School slate, gift of Anne Schofield under the Tax Incentives for the Arts Scheme, 1984. A9732

P164 — iPad tablet computer, ex-Museum 2013. 2013/130/1

SELECTED BIBLIOGRAPHY

Atkinson, P *Computer*, Reaktion Books, New York, 2010

Bellini, M and Vaughan, G, *Mario Bellini: architect and designer*, National Gallery of Victoria, Melbourne, 2003

Deutcher Werkbund, *Form without ornament*, Deutcher Werkbund, Germany, 1924

Dresser, C, *Studies in design*, Gibbs Smith, England, 1874

Esslinger, H, *Keep It Simple: The Early Design Years of Apple*, Arnoldsche Art Publishers, Stuttgart, Germany, 2013

Gregotti, V, Bosoni, G, Andrea De Giorgi, M, *Il disegno del prodotto industriale Italia 1860–1980*, Milano Electa, Milan, 1986

Kahney, L, *Inside Steve's brain*, Portfolio, New York, 2008

Klier, H, von King, P, Shapira, N H A, *Design process: Olivetti, 1908–1978*, Frederick S Wight Art Gallery, University of California, Los Angeles, California, 1979 Frederick S Wight Art Gallery/ Olivetti, 1979

Kunkel, P, *Apple design: The work of the Apple Industrial Design group*, Watson-Guptill Publications, New York, 1997

Lally, E, 'At home with computers', *Materialising culture*, Berg, Oxford and New York, 2002

Lashinsky, A, *Inside Apple*, John Murray Publishers, London, 2012

Levy, S, *The perfect thing: how the iPod shuffles commerce, culture, and coolness*, Simon & Schuster, New York, 2007

Linzmayer, O, *Apple confidential 2.0: The definitive history of the world's most colourful company*, No Starch Press, San Francisco, 2004

Lovell, S, *Dieter Rams: as little design as possible*, Phaidon, London, New York, 2011

Lucie-Smith, E, *A history of industrial design* Phaidon, Oxford, 1983

Lupton, E, Abbott Miller, J, *The ABCs of [triangle, square, circle]: the Bauhaus and design theory*, Thames and Hudson, London, 1993

Marcus, G H, *Functionalist design: an ongoing history* Prestel, Munich, 1995

Marquart, C, *Industrial culture, industrial design: a piece of German economic and design history, the founder members of the Association of German Industrial Designers*, Ernst & Sohn, Berlin,1993

McCarty, C, Weiley, S, Bellini, M, *Mario Bellini designer*, Museum of Modern Art New York, 1987

Moggridge, B, *Designing interactions*, MIT Press, Cambridge, 2007

Montreal Museum of Fine Arts *Il modo italiano: Italian design and avant-garde in the 20th century*, Montreal Museum of Fine Arts, Montreal, 2006

Museum für Kunst und Gewerbe Hamburg *Apple design*, Ostfildern, Berlin; Hatje Cantz, Gestalten Verlag, 2011

Rams, D, Ueki-Polet, K, Klemp, K, *Less and more: the design ethos of Dieter Rams*, Design Museum London, MAK Frankfurt San Francisco Museum of Modern Art, Gestalten, Berlin, 2011

Sparke, P, *Design in Italy 1870 to the present*, Abbeville Press, New York, 1988

Sparke, P, Antonelli, P, *Japanese design* (MoMA design series), Museum of Modern Art, New York, 2009

ABOUT THE CONTRIBUTORS

CAMPBELL BICKERSTAFF is the curator of information technology at the Museum of Applied Arts and Sciences in Sydney, Australia. In that role he has embraced an approach to collecting, researching and publishing with the intent to highlight the abstract connections between the technological development of material culture, its adoption and use, and the phenomenological association to the aesthetics of objects.

SEAMUS BYRNE is an Australian technology journalist. He is currently the editor of CNET Australia and acts as a regular technology commentator for the Seven Network and the ABC. Over the past decade he has won technology journalism awards for his coverage of both consumer technology and the video games industry. His particular interests lie in the long term future of technology and its impact on society and culture, and also paleofuturism, the study of the history of our attempts to predict the future.

JESSE ADAMS STEIN is a researcher specialising in the relationship between technology, labour, and design. She recently completed a PhD at UTS, which focused on the history of the NSW Government Printing Office, with an emphasis on technology, gender and working life. In 2009 she graduated with a MA in design history from the Art Institute of Chicago, and in 2005 she was awarded the University Medal for art theory at UNSW. Jesse teaches design history, cultural studies and the history of technology.

MARIO BELLINI lives and works in Milan. His activities range from architecture and urban design to furniture and industrial design. Internationally renowned, he is winner among others of eight Compasso d'Oro, and prestigious architecture awards including the Medaglia d'Oro, conferred on him by the President of the Italian Republic. He has given talks in the great cultural centres of the world and was editor of *Domus*. His work can be found in the collections of major art museums, including MoMA, New York, which has 25 of his works in its permanent design collection. He has had countless exhibitions in his name in Italy and internationally. From the 1980s onwards he has designed projects such as Portello Trade Fair quarter, Milan; Exhibition Centre, Villa Erba, Lake Como; Tokyo Design Centre, Japan; Natuzzi America Headquarters, USA; Essen Trade Fair, Germany; National Gallery of Victoria, Melbourne; Deutsche Bank Headquarters, Frankfurt; Verona Forum complex; History of Bologna Museum; the new Department of Islamic Art at the Louvre, Paris; and the Milan Convention Centre at Milan Trade Fair.

ACKNOWLEDGMENTS

MAAS would like to thank our generous donors and lenders who have contributed to the Museum's collection and the *Interface* exhibition; guest authors Jesse Adams Stein and Seamus Byrne; and Mario Bellini for agreeing to be interviewed for this book. The Museum also acknowledges the following staff who have contributed to the project: Campbell Bickerstaff, *Interface* curator; Dolla Merrillees, Director, Curatorial, Collections and Exhibitions; Judith Matheson, Editorial & Publishing Manager; Matthew Connell, Senior Curator, Technology and Innovation; Iwona Hetherington, Rights and Permissions; Sotha Bourn and Marinco Kojdanovski, MAAS photographers; Melanie Cariss and Karla Bo Johnson, MAAS editors; Vanessa Mack, volunteer researcher, Ross Clendinning, *Interface* Project Coordinator and the *Interface* exhibition team.